JASPER F. CROPSEY

Artist and Architect

JASPER

F. CROPSEY

Artist and Architect

Paintings, Drawings, and Photographs
from the Collections of the Newington-Cropsey
Foundation and The New-York Historical Society

Essays by Ella M. Foshay & Barbara Finney
Catalog by Mishoe Brennecke

THE NEW-YORK HISTORICAL SOCIETY, NEW YORK

Published in conjunction with the exhibition *Jasper F. Cropsey: Artist and Architect* held at
The New-York Historical Society from October 28, 1987, to February 14, 1988

Edited by Jacolyn A. Mott
Designed by Bruce Campbell
Typeset and printed by Meriden-Stinehour Press

PHOTOGRAPH CREDITS

All color photographs are by Glenn Castellano and all black-and-white photographs are by the
Newington-Cropsey Foundation, with the exception of the following:

Gamma One Conversions, pp. 2, 53
Museum of Fine Arts, Boston, pp. 140, 142, 144
Newington-Cropsey Foundation, pp. 61, 111
New York Public Library, p. 21
Woodmere Art Museum, Philadelphia, p. 25

LIBRARY OF CONGRESS CATALOGING-IN-PUBLICATION DATA

Cropsey, Jasper Francis, 1823–1900.
Jasper F. Cropsey (1823–1900), artist and architect.

Bibliography: p. 171
"Published in conjunction with the exhibition . . . held at The New-York Historical Society
from October 28, 1987, to February 14, 1988"—T.p. verso.
1. Cropsey, Jasper Francis, 1823–1900—Catalogs.
I. Foshay, Ella M., 1948–   . II. Finney, Barbara.
III. Brennecke, Mishoe, 1962–   . IV. Newington-Cropsey Foundation. V. New-York Historical Society.
VI. Title.
N6537.C746A4   1987   709'.2'4   87–18589
ISBN 0–916141–00–4 (pbk.)

Cover: Detail of *The Millennial Age*, 1854, oil on canvas
Collection of the Newington-Cropsey Foundation

Title page: Castle Garden, New York City, 1859, oil on canvas
Collection of The New-York Historical Society

Page 31 : Summer, 1855, oil on canvas
Collection of the Newington-Cropsey Foundation

Contents

Edward L. Mooney, *Jasper F. Cropsey*, ca. 1847, oil on canvas, 31 x 26 in. Newington-Cropsey Foundation.

Foreword

Nearly sixty-five years ago the Society acquired its first landscape painting by Jasper F. Cropsey. Since then additional works by the distinguished Hudson River school painter have supplemented the Society's holdings. Today we are delighted to join with Mrs. John C. Newington and the Newington-Cropsey Foundation to mount an exhibition that surveys the creative accomplishment of the artist.

Since 1609, when the English navigator Henry Hudson sailed up the river, travellers have recounted in their diaries, journals, and tales the beguiling, mysterious, and dazzling beauty of the Hudson River scenery. Today the enchantment of the Hudson River and the engaging vitality of its cities and towns both delight the eye and dramatically recall the history and legends attached to the 375-year development of New York.

On the porch of Jasper F. Cropsey's carefully preserved house and studio at 49 Washington Avenue, Hastings-on-Hudson, our eyes have a riveting glimpse of the Hudson River and the Palisades, which frequently stirred his artistic imagination during every season and produced several large and impressive landscapes.

This exhibition is the fruit of engaging and congenial visits and conversations with Mrs. John C. Newington during the past several years. It is also the culmination of many months of research, planning, and design by the Society's curator of painting and sculpture, Ella M. Foshay, and her associates. We all are grateful to Mrs. John C. Newington for allowing us to display so many of the treasures in the collection of the Newington-Cropsey Foundation.

JAMES B. BELL
Director

Acknowledgments

From beginning to end, the catalog and exhibition devoted to the work of Jasper F. Cropsey have been a collaboration between The New-York Historical Society and the Newington-Cropsey Foundation. Every step of the way, Mrs. John C. Newington, Cropsey's great-granddaughter and trustee of the foundation, provided support, guidance, and gentle good humor. Florence Levins, administrator of the foundation's collections, shared with me her knowledge of the artist's life and work. She directed my research through the important manuscript, library, and study collections at Cropsey's house and studio at Hastings-on-Hudson, New York. Theresa Bernert, caretaker-in-residence, always made me and my colleagues welcome and comfortable.

Every exhibition at The New-York Historical Society depends upon the cooperation and support of staff members throughout the institution. My thanks go to all of them, although I am unable to mention every name. Karen Stiefel, coordinator of exhibitions, directed her extraordinary and limitless talents to shaping and developing all facets of the project. Monique Richards, research associate, refined the catalog's text with care; and Christine Oaklander, assistant, was unfailingly helpful.

The catalog entries devoted to Cropsey's paintings represent only a small portion of Mishoe Brennecke's contribution. As research assistant, she gathered information, supervised photography, and developed the chronology and bibliography for the catalog. Barbara Finney has defined Cropsey's architectural accomplishments, a component of his artistic career that deserves recognition. Thanks go to Stephen Zeitz for his precise review of the books in the artist's library. Jacolyn A. Mott molded the structure and edited the prose of the catalog's text with sensitivity and grace. The design reflects the aesthetic expertise of Bruce Campbell. Glenn Castellano deserves praise for the sharp focus and precise color of the illustrations.

Staff members at other institutions supported the work. The Archives of American Art and the Museum of the City of New York accommodated numerous research visits and inquiries. Kevin Stayton, associate curator of decorative arts at The Brooklyn Museum, and Alice Cooney Frelinghuysen, associate curator of American decorative arts at The Metropolitan Museum of Art, reviewed the furnishings at Cropsey's home.

Earlier publications provided the foundation of information about Jasper Cropsey. Recent catalogs devoted to the artist's drawings and watercolors in the Newington-Cropsey Foundation's collection, prepared by Kenneth W. Maddox and Carrie Rebora, respectively, offered useful insights into the artist's approach to those media and the development of his skills in using them. To the ground-breaking scholarship of William S. Talbot, we are all indebted.

E. M. F.

JASPER F. CROPSEY
Artist and Architect

Fig. 1: Jasper and Maria Cropsey as they were dressed when presented to Queen Victoria, June 27, 1861, photographs, undated. Newington-Cropsey Foundation.

Jasper F. Cropsey: Painter

BY ELLA M. FOSHAY

The Newington-Cropsey Foundation's collection of the work of Jasper F. Cropsey (1823–1900) demonstrates a rare sustained appreciation of a nineteenth-century American artist's accomplishments by subsequent generations of his family. Although there were a number of auctions of Cropsey's works and possessions during and after his lifetime, a substantial amount of important material was retained by his descendants despite the vagaries of taste and economic fortune. The artist's two granddaughters, Isabel Steinschneider and Constance Mead, were responsible for preserving this archival treasure.

For the last fifteen years of his life, from 1885 to 1900, Jasper Cropsey and his wife, Maria, lived in a house called Ever Rest in Hastings-on-Hudson, New York. In 1887, one of their daughters, Rose, and her husband, Conrad Wack, were killed in a train accident. Their children, Isabel and Constance, aged six and eight years, were sent east from California to live with their grandparents. Thus, during their formative years, the two girls developed a strong sense of their rich artistic and cultural heritage. Isabel, in particular, "saved everything," according to her daughter Barbara (Mrs. John C. Newington), "even the court costume that Cropsey wore when he and Maria were presented to Queen Victoria" (fig. 1).[1] Isabel married William Steinschneider in 1916 and continued to live at Ever Rest. She preserved a great deal of important historical and artistic material about Jasper F. Cropsey. Most of his oil paintings had been sold during his lifetime or shortly thereafter, and only a few have come down through the family. Those that never left the collection are *Stateroom on Ship en Route to England* (cat. no. 25), *Wooded Landscape* (cat. no. 36), and *Study for "Starrucca Viaduct—Autumn"* (cat. no. 26). Isabel and her husband added to the collection with two purchases: *Days of Elizabeth* (cat. no. 13) and a series of Civil War studies (cat. no. 30).

It was, however, in the safekeeping of other materials that the Steinschneiders contributed most to our understanding of the artist's development. All of Cropsey's works on paper, including watercolors, architectural drawings, and pencil sketches, remained in his possession and were preserved in his studio at Ever Rest after his death. Some furniture that his family believes was designed by him and portions of his library were also kept.

Like his contemporaries, Cropsey collected visual models in the form of engravings of works by other artists. Small and large clippings in many portfolios, which have been preserved at Ever Rest, record his preference for certain artists, types of subject matter, visual perspectives, and pictorial styles. Probably Cropsey purchased many of these engravings during his two trips to Europe. While there are a few religious subjects and some genre scenes, most of them record landscapes of the Old World, often with evocative classical ruins or romantic medieval castles. The greatest number of engravings based upon the work of a single artist are those after J. M. W. Turner (1775–1851), the British artist with whom critics on both sides of the Atlantic often compared Cropsey.[2]

Almost all of the Cropsey oil paintings that were owned by his family had been sold by 1906 when the remaining works in his studio were auctioned by the Silo Galleries in New York. It is therefore to the credit of Cropsey's great-granddaughter Barbara Steinschneider Newington and her husband, John C. Newington, that the important collection of oil paintings in this exhibition have been gathered together. Throughout their years together, after their marriage in 1948, the Newingtons bought important Cropsey oils with the intention of putting together a collection that would illuminate the artist's achievement. Their earliest acquisition, made in 1951, was *Church, Stoke Poges* (cat. no. 35). The most recent addition to the collection is *Lake Scene, Franconia Notch* (cat. no. 32), purchased early in 1987. In 1979, the Newingtons established the Newington-Cropsey Foundation to preserve the artist's studio and its contents for future generations.

The oil paintings from the foundation's collection, as they are represented in this exhibition, date from every creative decade of the artist's life. Landscapes, of course, predominate. Some of the sites depicted in these landscapes were of special importance to Cropsey at certain stages of his personal and artistic life. A very early work, painted when he was twenty, shows the farm on Staten Island where he was born in 1823 (fig. 2). Reminiscing some years later, he noted that both his parents were natives of the island and that the best of his childhood landscape sketches was made from the window of the farmhouse when he was about ten years old.[3] *Cottage on Upper Greenwood Lake* (fig. 3) is a scene in the vicinity of Maria Cooley's home. Cropsey had met her there earlier, and he married her in 1847, the year that this picture was painted.

Naples (fig. 4), a picturesque Italian road scene, captures the immediacy of the artist's experience. His first trip to Europe, from 1847 to 1849, was spent mostly in Italy; and he was inspired throughout his career by its landscape, history, and art. While traveling there with his bride, he visited such important sites as Capri, Lake Nemi, and Paestum and made sketches that would serve as models for later finished compositions. The Cropseys enjoyed the company of other American artists during the trip, namely, the portraitist Thomas Hicks (1823–1890),

Fig. 2: *Cropsey Farm, Staten Island*, 1843 (cat. no. 2). Newington-Cropsey Foundation.

Fig. 3: *Cottage on Upper Greenwood Lake*, 1847 (cat. no. 4). Newington-Cropsey Foundation.

Fig. 4: *Naples*, 1848 (cat. no. 6). Newington-Cropsey Foundation.

the classical sculptor William Wetmore Story (1819–1895), and the poet-painter Christopher
P. Cranch (1813–1892).[4]

From 1856 to 1863, the Cropseys lived in England. Their Atlantic crossing is recorded in
a small, informal oil sketch entitled *Stateroom on Ship en Route to England* (fig. 5). A quiet domestic
scene, it shows Maria in the background, reading, and her two daughters in the foreground,
sewing and drinking tea in their quarters on the ocean liner. In England Cropsey painted and
exhibited important works that established his reputation abroad. He also made sketches of
specific scenes to use in his later work. The Newington-Cropsey Foundation's collection has
several paintings of the English country church at Stoke Poges that was made famous in Thomas
Gray's "Elegy Written in a Country Churchyard," published in 1751. The rendering of *Church,
Stoke Poges*, 1872 (fig. 6), reflects Cropsey's long-standing interest in structures and architectural
details. A later painting, done in 1883 as part of a series of the four seasons, depicts the church
as a romantic symbol in a summer landscape (cat. no. 44). These works were probably based
on sketches made during the artist's residence in England.

As the collection indicates, however, it is landscapes of the New World, not the Old, that
predominate in the oeuvre of Jasper F. Cropsey. These are his greatest creative achievement.
Like the other members of the Hudson River school, Cropsey was drawn to the lakes, rivers,
mountains, and valleys of the northeastern United States for their pristine beauty and their

Fig. 5: *Stateroom on Ship en Route to England*, 1856 (cat. no. 25). Newington-Cropsey Foundation.

Fig. 6: *Church, Stoke Poges*, 1872 (cat. no. 35). Newington-Cropsey Foundation.

Fig. 7: *Niagara*, 1853 (cat. no. 15). Newington-Cropsey Foundation.

potential to fulfill the desire for a national art in this country. He was attracted not only to the pastoral stretches of the Hudson valley where the banks were low and the river smooth but also to the rugged edges of the Palisades and the mountainous surrounds of Echo Lake, New Hampshire. He recorded the encroachments of technological progress, for good or ill, in a number of country scenes. A valley in Wayne County, Pennsylvania, for example, embraces an unobtrusive Erie Railroad viaduct in the *Study for "Starrucca Viaduct—Autumn"* (cat. no. 26). Cropsey's landscapes demonstrate his interest in the particular effects of atmosphere, weather, and cloud formations and his desire to capture both the visual and affective qualities of the changing seasons. The undisputed beauty and infinite variety of nature in America inspired Cropsey and other artists of his generation to observe it closely, explore it, make sketches of sites and details, and, ultimately, canonize it in large-scale paintings. These paintings were a tribute to the potential of America's landscape, as a reflection of its creator, to bring its inhabitants closer to God and to help forge a national identity sanctified by this connection.

Two major compositions by Jasper Cropsey in the Newington-Cropsey Foundation's col-

Fig. 8: *The Millennial Age*, 1854 (cat. no. 17). Newington-Cropsey Foundation.

lection, both dating from the early 1850s, suggest the complexity of the artist's responses to nature and his interpretations of it. *Niagara* (fig. 7), painted in 1853, and *The Millennial Age* (fig. 8), produced the following year, provide a study in contrast. *Niagara* records a specific New World site that Cropsey had visited and recreated in a naturalistic style. *The Millennial Age* is an idealized conception of the Old World. The figures are symbolic, the subject is taken from the Bible, and the setting is imaginary, although the details of the landscape have been studied from nature. Thus, these paintings represent the two sides of the complex philosophical debate that engaged many nineteenth-century landscape painters: the importance of the real versus the ideal in the representation of nature. As these paintings show, Cropsey devoted equal attention to both modes during the 1850s, in spite of the fact that objective representations of real places had been the favored approach to landscape art for some time.[5]

In a lecture delivered before the New York Art Re-Union in 1845, he emphasized the importance of nature as the primary source of inspiration for the best landscape painting of the past and for the young artists of his own day. "I find in recalling to mind those that have the greatest works (I have reference to LANDSCAPE only)," he said, "have been the most attentive to nature—have gained their principles in the art, and their feeling for color from her; their best works or the works that met with the most admiration, are their nearest approaches to nature."[6]

Thomas Cole (1801–1848), the American landscape painter most admired by Cropsey, visited Niagara Falls before embarking on an extended European tour in 1829. Like many other American artists traveling abroad, Cole feared that a kind of loss of innocence might take place amid the landscapes of the Old World. "I cannot think of going to Europe without having seen [Niagara Falls]," he wrote. "I wish to take a 'last, lingering look' at our wild scenery. I shall endeavour to impress its features so strongly on my mind that, in the midst of the fine scenery of other countries, their grand and beautiful peculiarities shall not be erased."[7]

By the time of Cole's visit, the falls had awed explorers and artists for two hundred years.[8] In the 1850s, when Cropsey painted *Niagara*, the site was attracting tourists from near and far. During an era characterized by an optimistic national spirit, the power and splendor of the falls symbolized for many the young democracy's grand destiny. A testimony to the early acceptance of Niagara Falls as the landscape icon of America can be found in an engraving of 1800. Entitled *Emblem of America* (fig. 9), it shows a female personification of America, carrying an American flag and leaning gracefully on the sturdy tombstone of George Washington. The stone also serves as a bolster for the weight of another national emblem—the American Indian. A clear rendering of Niagara Falls provides the setting. Together with George Washington, the American Indians, and the stars and stripes of the national flag, the great falls symbolized what was unique about America.

Cropsey's painting *Niagara* was developed from sketches made during his first trip to the site in 1852. He selected a point of view on the American side that stressed the height and breadth of the cataract. Suspending the viewer over a slippery rock in the foreground, Cropsey projected the physical presence and potential danger of this magnificent volume of water. In fact, in *Niagara*, he recreated his personal experience, making sketches at the site. A local real estate agent had called Cropsey's attention to a fallen rock in the Niagara River not far from the base of the falls. In a letter to his wife, he described wading with some difficulty to the spot "amid the spray" which, during his subsequent sketching, became "so dense as to cover me as with a thick fog and fall like a shower upon my work."[9]

Cropsey's landscapes were most often praised for their close attention to nature, rather than for the complex conception that *The Millennial Age* represents. Two works exhibited at the National Academy of Design were applauded as "extraordinary" by a reviewer for the *Literary World*. He attributed their fine quality to the artist's reliance upon the direct experience of nature. "Mr. Cropsey is one of the few among our young landscape painters," the reviewer

Fig. 9: Unidentified artist, *An Emblem of America*, 1800, mezzotint. Print Collection, Miriam & Ira D. Wallach Division of Art, Prints and Photographs, The New York Public Library, Astor, Lenox and Tilden Foundations.

claimed, "who go directly to nature for their materials. . . .He aims to reproduce within the limits of his appliances something akin to the productions of the prime old master, Nature, and so long as he confines himself to this school he is safe."[10] Cropsey entreated artists not to take nature for granted but rather to educate their eyes and aesthetic faculties by studying closely the particularities of their natural surroundings. In 1855, shortly after painting *Niagara* and *The Millennial Age*, he published "Up among the Clouds," in which he called the sky "a dome of treasure" and used his precise powers of observation and description to catalog its various aspects. Contrasting the "delicate fleecy, fibrous wave-ribbed character" of distant cirrus clouds with "grand masses of dreamy [cumulus] forms floating by each other," he demonstrated his acute perception of the particular effects of atmosphere.[11] It seems that in painting *Niagara* he selected the site on the river that offered the best perspective of the sky as well as the impressive cataract. Recalling the painting many years later, Cropsey said that it should be "admired for its silvery and clear atmosphere. . . [t]he purity and beauty of the blue

Fig. 10: Detail of *The Millennial Age*, 1854 (cat. no. 17). Newington-Cropsey Foundation.

sky, with its fleecy clouds, and the longer bank of cumuli cloud which is formed by so much vapor."[12]

The landscape in *The Millennial Age* (also called *The Golden Age*) is entirely different from the quintessentially American scene in *Niagara*. The site is clearly not the New World but the Old. It is not a specific place but a generalized Arcadia probably formed by a combination of European places of historic and artistic interest that Cropsey had visited during his first trip abroad. Moreover, the dominant feature of the composition is a work not of nature but of art.[13]

Fig. 11: Sketch for *The Millennial Age*, ca. 1854, pencil with touches of white on paper, 9⅜ x 6⅛ in. Newington-Cropsey Foundation.

It is a monumental classical sculpture that combines Christian and pagan themes (figs. 10, 11).

The organization of *The Millennial Age* invites an analytical approach to the scene, whereas *Niagara* conveys the physical immediacy of the great falls. In *The Millennial Age*, the landscape is a stage set, securely framed by luxuriant palms at the left and right. Cropsey provides a comfortable foreground space for the viewer to enter and a gently winding path through the middle distance to the far city at the water's edge. There is time and space for contemplating the works of art, symbolic figures, and suggestive elements of nature along the way and for analyzing their implied comment on the relationship of art, civilization, religion, and nature.

In the complexity of narrative detail and the classical structure of the composition, *The Millennial Age* belongs to the tradition of historical allegory painted in the Grand Manner. This genre emphasized concept over direct perception in landscape painting and promoted the didactic role of art. The taste for this kind of painting was never strong in America, and by the 1850s it had certainly been superceded by a preference for the "view"—a painting based upon direct observation of a recognizable site. Cropsey's *Niagara*, for example, is a view magnified to a grand scale consistent with its subject. American scenes of quiet beauty, such as pastoral landscapes of the Hudson valley, and those of extraordinary grandeur, such as the Natural Bridge in Virginia or Niagara Falls, were favored by critics and patrons of the period.

The Millennial Age takes its title from the Book of Revelations in the Bible, which describes a thousand years of triumphant holiness on earth. That reference and the profusion of narrative detail in the painting make clear Cropsey's didactic purpose. The carved monument at the left, which is an altar, is crowned with sculptured figures of a lion, a lamb, a calf, and a child. Beneath the slab that supports them is a pedestal encircled by classical maidens carrying palms, traditional symbols of peace. Centered on the front of the sculpture, two carved *putti* provide clues to the meaning of the allegory represented by the monument. One carries a Christian cross, sparkling in the sunlight; the other holds a banderole inscribed "On Earth Peace," which, being unfurled on the reverse side, reads backwards. Below the putti, at the base of the sculpture, is carved an open Bible, citing references to the Book of Isaiah: chapter two, verse four, on the left-hand page; and chapter eleven, verse six, on the right. These verses describe life on earth after the coming of the Messiah. They provide precise and evocative images of transformations that will occur in the civilized world and in nature during the Millennial Age. Following God's judgment, in the words of Cropsey's own Cottage Bible of 1834, people "shall beat their swords into plowshares, and their spears into pruning-hooks: nation shall not lift up sword against nation, neither shall they learn war any more."[14] Harmony will likewise prevail in the animal kingdom. According to Isaiah, "The wolf also shall dwell with the lamb, and the leopard shall lie down with the kid, and the calf and the young lion and the fatling together; and a little child shall lead them." The explanatory notes that accompany these verses in Cropsey's Bible

Fig. 12: *The Spirit of Peace*, 1851, oil on canvas, 44 x 67 in. Woodmere Art Museum, Philadelphia, bequest of Charles Knox Smith.

compare this land of peace and happiness with that described by earlier writers: "The Greek and Latin poets have painted their *golden age* in very beautiful colours, but the exquisite imagery of Isaiah stands unequalled and inimitable."[15]

Shortly before painting *The Millennial Age*, Cropsey treated the same theme in *The Spirit of War*, 1851 (National Gallery of Art, Washington), and *The Spirit of Peace*, 1851 (Woodmere Art Museum, Philadelphia). It is clear that he borrowed many symbols and narrative details from *The Spirit of Peace* (fig. 12) and reorganized and refined them in *The Millennial Age*.[16] The dominant element in both compositions is a classical monument (one, a temple; the other, an altar) in a landscape with exotic palm trees set in front of an open view of the sea on a calm, clear day. White lilies, traditional symbols of the Resurrection, grow in the foreground. In both pictures, there are shepherds tending their flocks, figures dancing and playing musical instruments, and a woman holding a distaff. These activities refer symbolically to the flourishing of the domestic and fine arts in the nurturing environment of a peaceful land. Cropsey described some specific concepts that he intended to project in *The Spirit of Peace*, which define equally well his intention

Fig. 13: James Smillie after Thomas Cole, *Dream of Arcadia*, 1850, engraving. Newington-Cropsey Foundation.

in *The Millennial Age*. He referred to the monument as a "Temple of Peace. . . occupying a commanding position and prospect over a fruitful country, growing city, and open sea." The palm trees and sweet-smelling flowers, he explained, provided "emblems of purity in peace and plenty." Domestic happiness and pastoral peace found expression in the pursuits of the Arcadian figures under "the sun of a cloudless day in a cloudless sky, leaving the new moon to renew by night the tale of happy and perpetual change that has followed the stern and desolate times of human strife. Man's peace is made with man and his creator."[17]

In *The Millennial Age*, Cropsey combined references to pre-Christian civilization with obvious Christian emblems to create his painted allegory. According to the artist, this dream of harmony, productivity, and peace had already been achieved from time to time when conditions were right. It required civilized man to suppress hostility, aggression, and their destructive consequences in order to reclaim an idyllic world, innocent of evil. As Isaiah said, "A little child shall lead them." Thus, Cropsey put a child at the pinnacle of his highly symbolic monument.

How can we explain Cropsey's continuing interest in the kind of allegorical art that is represented by his painting *The Millennial Age*? Certainly his long-standing admiration for

Thomas Cole contributed to it. Cropsey shared Cole's attraction to the evocative landscapes of Italy for their allusion to history and literature. Furthermore, Cole had continued to paint both views and compositions until the end of his life in 1848, and Cropsey no doubt admired this versatility. Even after Cole died, Cropsey felt his presence strongly during a visit to Cole's Catskill studio. "Though the man had departed," wrote Cropsey, "yet he has left a spell behind him that is not broken."[18] Although there may have been more, two engravings by Cole remain in the Newington-Cropsey Foundation's collection at Hastings-on-Hudson. Both are based upon allegorical compositions. One is *Old Age* from the series The Voyage of Life, and the other is James Smillie's 1850 engraving of Cole's *Dream of Arcadia* (fig. 13).[19] It is very likely that Cole's rendering of Arcadia inspired Cropsey to select the subject for *The Millennial Age*.

The specifically moral and Christian themes that Cropsey included in *The Millennial Age* reflected his personal religious convictions. His letters are filled with allusions to his profound Christian faith and its impact on his approach to nature and art. He felt God close at hand in the beauties of his surroundings, and this belief encouraged him to observe the smallest details: "[T]he voice of God came to me through every motionless leaf, on every blade of grass — the odor of the flower and in every breath of air I drew."[20] In Cropsey's view, however, perception alone did not create an artist. Moral considerations were important, too. In fact, he once asserted that "no eminently moral, and refined work of art could be produced by an immoral, or loose-thinking man (and I'll take the liberty to add, woman)."[21] Therefore, Cropsey's selection of a Biblical subject with strong moral and religious implications for *The Millennial Age* depended, in part, upon his spiritual and ethical beliefs.

The Millennial Age was one of a number of allegorical compositions that Cropsey painted in the 1850s.[22] It was during this period that he traveled abroad to further his education in art and to improve his technical skills by studying the works of the Old Masters. Like Samuel F. B. Morse (1791–1872) and Thomas Cole, Cropsey aspired to compete with the accomplishments of the masters of the Renaissance and the ancient classical world.[23] His studies abroad convinced him to pursue the intellectual branch of art — allegorical painting. He wrote: "I have always been impressed with the idea that an artist to do justice to himself and his art should seek to express on his canvas the highest intellectual expressions, adding thereto all the refinement of poetry, and a well guided imagination. His thoughts should be pure and noble and the style simple but firm and I trust that my works and self may be worthy of it."[24]

The old world of art and history and the new world of nature and possibility were equally compelling inspirations to Jasper F. Cropsey. He drew upon both sources with no sense of conflict. They enriched his thematic vocabulary and gave variety to his compositions. Cropsey was able to respond to the landscapes and ruins of Europe for their physical beauty and their connections to history and religion, which were so important to his intellectual and spiritual life. *The Millennial Age* is the creative embodiment of this facet of Cropsey's sensibility. In *Niagara*, he portrayed the raw grandeur of a New World landscape and demonstrated its potential for creating a national art. With no direct allusions to religious, moral, or aesthetic convictions, the painting is, nonetheless, a reflection of Cropsey's complex ideas about nature in America. The pristine and powerful appearance of this dramatic landscape was the direct handiwork of the Creator and may therefore have seemed to Cropsey to be the perfect setting for the coming of a new millennial age.

NOTES

1. Mrs. John C. Newington, Jasper Cropsey's great-granddaughter, kindly provided me with a family genealogy and her personal recollections of the contribution of family members to the archives of the artist at Hastings-on-Hudson, New York.

2. A review of Cropsey's *Starrucca Vale*, 1862 (now unlocated), extolled its fine detail and exuberant color, remarking: "A student of nature so faithful to his task as Cropsey and with a pencil so fearless, may rest easy about the reputation of his works, which, like those of Turner, may stir up the critics of the present, yet be worshipped by the Ruskins of the future." Quoted in Henry T. Tuckerman, *Book of the Artists* (New York: S. P. Putnam and Sons, 1870), p. 538.

3. Jasper F. Cropsey, "Reminiscences of My Own Time" (1846), MS, coll. Brown Reinhardt, Newark, Del., typescript, p. 1, NCF. Written for C. E. Lester's *Artists of America* (New York, 1846) but not included.

4. University of Maryland Art Gallery, College Park, *Jasper F. Cropsey, 1823–1900: A Retrospective View of America's Painter of Autumn* (1968), exhib. cat. by Peter Bermingham, p. 18. Tuckerman noted that "early in the summer [1848], accompanied by his wife, [Cropsey] passed on to Naples, and spent the summer at Sorrento and Amalfi, living in the house with Story, the sculptor, and near C. P. Cranch, and visiting the temples of Paestum in their company." *Book of the Artists*, p. 535.

5. "In 1825, the tide of taste in America had begun to shift, from the idealized composition of the late eighteenth and early nineteenth centuries, to a new tendency towards objectivity which was characterized by a taste for the specific in nature and art." Barbara Deutsch [Novak], "Cole and Durand, Criticism and Patronage: A Study of American Taste in Landscape, 1825–65" (Ph.D. diss., Radcliffe College, 1957), p. 27.

6. J. Cropsey, "Some Reflections on Natural Art: An Address for the New York Art Re-Union" (Gaylords Bridge, Conn., August 24, 1845), MS, coll. Brown Reinhardt, Newark, Del., typescript, p. 4, NCF.

7. Thomas Cole to Robert Gilmor, April 26, 1829, quoted in Louis L. Noble, *The Life and Works of Thomas Cole* (Cambridge: Belknap Press of Harvard University Press, 1964), p. 72. In her essay entitled "An American Icon," Elizabeth McKinsey cites a poem by Cole that further expresses his nationalistic reading of Niagara Falls. The poem and the essay appear in Corcoran Gallery of Art, Washington, *Niagara: Two Centuries of Changing Attitudes, 1697–1901*, 1985, exhib. cat. by Jeremy E. Adamson, p. 92.

8. The first image of Niagara Falls was an engraving of 1697 that was based upon a written description of the site by a missionary priest, Father Louis Hennepin. It appeared in his widely read travel book entitled *Nouvelle Découverte d'un très grand pays Situé dans l'Amérique, entre le Nouveau Mexique et la Mer Glaciale* (Utrecht, 1697). See Corcoran Gallery (1985), p. 17.

9. J. Cropsey to Maria Cropsey, August 16, 1852, coll. Brown Reinhardt, Newark, Del., typescript, NCF.

10. *Literary World* 15 (May 15, 1847), pp. 347–48.

11. J. Cropsey, "Up among the Clouds," *Crayon* 2 (August 8, 1855), pp. 79–80. Barbara Novak analyzed this essay in detail and called it "a provocative mix of observation, poetry, esthetics, and science." *Nature and Culture: American Landscape and Painting, 1825–1875* (New York: Oxford University Press, 1980), p. 87.

12. J. Cropsey to John W. Kitchell, Nov. 1, 1897, John W. Kitchell Papers, microfilm, roll 1356, Archives of American Art, Smithsonian Institution, Washington.

13. "This altar group," according to William S. Talbot, whose publications constitute the primary scholarship on Cropsey's work, "is certainly one of the most singular pieces of sculpture ever conceived by an American painter." *Jasper F. Cropsey, 1823–1900* (Ph.D. diss., Institute of Fine Arts, New York University, 1972; published New York: Garland Publishing, 1977), p. 29.

14. *The Cottage Bible and Family Expositor . . . To Which are Added, the References and Marginal Readings of the Polyglott Bible, Together with Original Notes, and Selections from Bagster's Comprehensive Bible, and Other Standard Works. . . .* (Hartford: D. F. Robinson and H. F. Sumner, 1834), p. 739.

15. Ibid., pp. 747–48 nn. bottom of page.

16. Talbot (1972) notes the relationship between *The Spirit of Peace* and *The Millennial Age*, p. 108.

17. Cropsey's detailed descriptions of the allegorical program for *The Spirit of War* and *The Spirit of Peace* appeared in a letter addressed to Mr. M. (probably one of his patrons—E. P. Mitchell or George McGrath) and dated May 12, 1852, Miscellaneous Letters, Diaries, Sketches, and Memorandums of Jasper Francis Cropsey (cited hereafter as Cropsey Papers), NCF, microfilm, roll 336, Archives of American Art.

18. J. Cropsey to M. Cropsey, July 7, 1850, coll. Brown Reinhardt, Newark, Del., typescript, NCF.

19. Thomas Cole's painting of the *Dream of Arcadia* was engraved by James Smillie (1807–1885) and published by the American Art-Union for distribution to its members in 1850. In a letter to Asher B. Durand (1796–1886) in 1838, Cole had expressed his plan to treat this subject: "I intend to paint a scene, or a couple of scenes, in Arcadia, (of course in the golden age,) and I know not what else I might do if the sheet was large enough." Quoted in Noble (1964), p. 186.

20. J. Cropsey to fiancée, Maria Cooley, July 4, 1846, coll. Brown Reinhardt, Newark, Del., typescript, NCF.

21. In a letter to his fiancée, Nov. 22, 1846, ibid., Cropsey described an evening with a friend and patron, the artist John M. Falconer (1820–1903), in which the conversation concerned the subject of artists and their moral character.

22. Cropsey participated with several other artists to produce a series of sixteen scenes from John Bunyan's *Pilgrim's Progress. The Spirit of War* and *The Spirit of Peace* were also painted during this time. See Talbot (1972), pp. 27–28. *Days of Elizabeth* (cat. no. 13), inspired perhaps by the novels of Sir Walter Scott, is an example of Cropsey's interest in history painting during this period, as represented in the NCF collection.

23. Early in the nineteenth century, Samuel F. B. Morse was convinced during a stay in London that an artist must pursue the Grand Style of painting. In his view, only history painting (not portraits or even landscapes) could fulfill his ambition "to be among those who shall revive the splendor of the fifteenth century; to rival the genius of a Raphael, a Michael Angelo, or a Titian; my ambition is to be enlisted in the constellation of genius now rising in this country; I wish to shine, not by a light borrowed from them, but to strive to shine the brightest." Quoted in Oliver Larkin, *Samuel F. B. Morse and American Democratic Art* (Boston: Little, Brown and Co., 1954), p. 32.

24. J. Cropsey to Mr. M., May 12, 1852, Cropsey Papers, NCF.

CATALOG

Unless otherwise noted, all the paintings in this exhibition have been generously lent by the Newington-Cropsey Foundation.

Abbreviations used in the catalog entries are:

Arch. Am. Art	Archives of American Art, Smithsonian Institution, Washington, D.C.
Cropsey Papers	Miscellaneous Letters, Diaries, Sketches, and Memorandums of Jasper Francis Cropsey
NCF	Newington-Cropsey Foundation, Hastings-on-Hudson, N.Y.
NYHS	The New-York Historical Society

1. Temple of Minerva, Parthenon Restored, *ca. 1841*

Oil on paper, mounted on board, 5½ x 9¾ in.
Signed at lower left: J. F. Cropsey

EX COLLECTION
with a gallery in White Plains, N.Y.

Temple of Minerva, Parthenon Restored is the earliest work in oil by Jasper Cropsey in the Newington-Cropsey Foundation's collection. It was painted when he was about eighteen years old. From his unpublished "Reminiscences of My Own Time," it is clear that Cropsey was quite precocious as an artist and architect. When only twelve years old, he began work on a model of his home, which won for him a diploma at the Mechanics' Institute Fair in 1837. Soon after, Cropsey became an apprentice in the office of the New York architect Joseph Trench, where he received "lessons in landscape to enable [him] to put backgrounds to the architectural designs" and where he learned to use watercolors.[1] Sometime between 1837 and 1840, Cropsey won a second diploma, at the fair of the American Institute, for a watercolor entitled *The Temple of Minerva, Parthenon Restored*, ca. 1841. This unlocated sketch probably served as the model for the oil painting shown here.

Cropsey began painting in oil around 1841, and Trench encouraged him by providing canvases and paints and allowing the young artist to use his office as a studio before and after work. Proceeding in this fashion, Cropsey made his first oil paintings "both being copies from some of my watercolor drawings."[2] Perhaps *Temple of Minerva, Parthenon Restored* was one of these two early copies.

This oil painting shows the Acropolis in Athens, surrounded by mountains and valleys. The Parthenon, the ancient Greek temple dedicated to the goddess Athena—called Minerva by the Romans—is on the right-hand side of the promontory. The Temple of Athena Nike and the Propylaea are on the left. Because he had not visited Greece, Cropsey probably used an engraving of the Acropolis as a model for this scene.

1. Jasper F. Cropsey, "Reminiscences of My Own Time" (1846), MS, coll. Brown Reinhardt, Newark, Del., typescript, p. 5, NCF. An autobiographical essay written for C. E. Lester's *Artists of America* (New York, 1846) but not included.
2. Ibid., p. 6.

2. Cropsey Farm, Staten Island, *1843*

Oil on canvas, 6 x 7½ in.
Signed and dated at lower right: J. F. Cropsey/1843

EX COLLECTIONS
Mrs. J. A. Sharrott, Staten Island, N.Y.
with Richard Weimer Gallery, Darien, Conn., sold in 1986 to NCF.

One of Jasper Cropsey's early landscape paintings, *Cropsey Farm, Staten Island* shows his birthplace and childhood home. The farm, which consisted of a hundred acres of land, was located near Rossville.

A strongly horizontal design—marked by the split-rail fence that extends across the foreground and the wide zone of clear, bright sky at the top—indicates that the artist was experimenting with the elements of composition. The middle ground is dotted with houses, barns, fences, and grain bins, all reached by a curving dirt road. Trees on either side of the picture frame the view. The bright blue sky and gaily colored flowers add cheerfulness to the scene. Like the *Temple of Minerva, Parthenon Restored* (cat. no. 1), the *Cropsey Farm, Staten Island* shows the young artist grappling with technique. His handling of color and brushwork is still tentative. In his mature paintings the colors are better modulated and the forms increasingly firm.

3. Solitude, *1845*

Oil on canvas, 5¾ x 7½ in.
Signed and dated at lower left: J. F. Cropsey/1845

EX COLLECTIONS
probably John M. Falconer, Brooklyn, N.Y. (sale, Anderson Auction Company, New York,
April 28 and 29, 1904, no. 425).
with Lawrence Rau Gallery, Cincinnati, Ohio.
with Richard Weimer Gallery, Darien, Conn., sold in 1984 to NCF.

Jasper Cropsey's paintings of the mid-1840s are predominately landscapes, from areas close to New York City, especially New Jersey and his native Staten Island. The view in *Solitude*, painted in 1845, may be of Greenwood Lake in New Jersey. The title of the painting is accurate: the scene is uninhabited except for a bird sitting on a jagged, dead branch. Greens, golds, and browns with touches of red in the vines on the tree branches and pinks and purples in the glowing sunset establish the time as late afternoon in autumn and give an early indication of Cropsey's lifelong interest in recording specific times of day and seasons. The loose, rapid brushwork, the lack of detail, and the unusually narrow composition suggest that *Solitude* is a study for a larger painting.

Records of the sale of the estate of John M. Falconer in 1904 list "no. 425 Cropsey (Jasper F). 'Solitude, 1845.' Another autumnal study, of a deserted lake, mountains closing the background. In gilt frame, 14 in. x 11½ in."[1] Taking into account the size of the frame, the description of the Falconer study and its date match those of the painting shown here. Falconer, an artist himself and a close friend and patron of Cropsey, owned a number of his works and may well have admired *Solitude* in Cropsey's New York studio and bought it from him.

1. Anderson Auction Company, New York, April 28 and 29, 1904.

4. Cottage on Upper Greenwood Lake, *1847*

Oil on canvas, 13½ x 21½ in.
Signed and dated at lower left: J. F. Cropsey/1847

EX COLLECTION
with Sotheby Parke Bernet, New York, sold in 1979 to NCF.

Greenwood Lake, in northern New Jersey, was one of Jasper Cropsey's favorite sites during the 1840s and a location that he painted many times throughout his life. The lake was once called "Double Pond" because it is nearly divided by a large island, thus the designation "Upper Greenwood Lake" in the title of this painting.[1] Cropsey was introduced to the area by John P. Ridner, a New York art dealer. Also through Ridner, Cropsey met his future wife, Maria Cooley (1829–1906), whose family lived on Greenwood Lake in the town of West Milford. Evidently, Maria's parents encouraged Cropsey's visits. Her father, Isaac Cooley, offered to build a "painting room" for the artist.[2] It is not known whether or not the studio was ever built.

Cropsey began to exhibit views of Greenwood Lake as early as 1843 and had shown at least seven by the end of the decade. One of them won him election as an associate of the National Academy of Design in 1844 (*View in Orange County with Greenwood Lake in the Distance*, no. 68, now unlocated). *Cottage on Upper Greenwood Lake* is a scene of rural harmony, showing a cottage overlooking the lake, a young boy fishing in the foreground, a woman pumping water near the house, and a man tending the fields in the background. Peacefulness is echoed in the sunny landscape.

This quiet, happy scene was probably painted during the spring of 1847 when Cropsey was making plans for his wedding trip. It reflects his fond attachment to the area, as well as his joy over his forthcoming marriage to the young woman from Greenwood Lake.

1. J. Cropsey to John W. Kitchell, May 24, 1897, John W. Kitchell Papers, microfilm, roll 1356, Arch. Am. Art.
2. J. Cropsey to M. Cooley, March 30, 1846, and Nov. 4, 1845, also I. Cooley to J. Cropsey, April 24, 1846, coll. Brown Reinhardt, Newark, Del., typescripts, NCF. See William S. Talbot, *Jasper F. Cropsey, 1823–1900* (Ph.D. diss., Institute of Fine Arts, New York University, 1972; published New York: Garland Publishing, 1977), pp. 37–38.

5. Rugged Mountain Scene (Italian), 1847

Oil on canvas, 18¼ x 26 in.
Signed and dated at lower left: J. F. Cropsey/1847

EX COLLECTION
with Richard Weimer Gallery, Darien, Conn., sold in 1982 to NCF.

In late September of 1847, after a brief stay in England and a quick trip across the Continent, Jasper Cropsey and his wife, Maria, arrived in Italy. In Rome, they settled into Thomas Cole's former studio in the via Babuino. Soon afterwards, Cropsey painted *Rugged Mountain Scene (Italian)*. This treacherous mountain landscape recalls Cropsey's *View Near Rome*, also painted in 1847 in Rome (NYHS, on permanent loan from New York Public Library). In both paintings, Cropsey heightens the drama of an otherwise pastoral scene by the predominance of grand and gloomy mountains, foreboding storm clouds, and dramatic lighting.

Rugged Mountain Scene (Italian) shows an energetic, broad handling of paint that is appropriate to the rough terrain. The overall coloring of the painting is dark, with large areas of grays, greens, browns, and blacks. The range of mountains in the background provides a strong focus for the composition. A source of inspiration for these mountains may have been the Alps, through which Cropsey had recently journeyed, via the Simplon Pass, en route to Italy. Also, the jagged and snow-capped peaks are similar to ones found in the paintings of Thomas Cole. In Cole's *Saint John in the Wilderness*, 1827 (Wadsworth Atheneum, Hartford), a large outcropping silhouetted against clouds near the center of the composition bears a striking resemblance to the knob-shaped promontory in this painting by Cropsey. Dangerous-looking mountains dominate both scenes, and human figures are completely overwhelmed.

6. Naples, *1848*

Oil on canvas, 27⅜ x 43⅜ in.
Signed and dated at lower left: J. F. Cropsey/1848

REFERENCES
Cleveland Museum of Art, Munson-Williams-Proctor Institute, Utica, N.Y., and National Collection
of Fine Arts, Smithsonian Institution, Washington, traveling exhib., 1970–71,
Jasper F. Cropsey, 1823–1900, cat. by William S. Talbot, no. 6, p. 67, as *Bridge in Italy.*
William S. Talbot, *Jasper F. Cropsey, 1823–1900*, Ph.D. diss., Institute of Fine Arts, New York
University, 1972; published New York: Garland Publishing,
1977, no. 26, fig. 23, pp. 57–58, as *Bridge in Italy.*

EX COLLECTIONS
D. D. Brodek, New York (auction, American Art-Union, 1850, no. 135).
with Berry-Hill Galleries, New York, sold in 1956 to Mr. and Mrs. John C. Newington.

In the summer of 1848, the Cropseys stayed in the coastal region of southern Italy, where Jasper made sketching trips to Paestum, Salerno, Capri, Amalfi, and Naples and worked occasionally with fellow American artists William Wetmore Story and Christopher P. Cranch. Part of that summer was spent in Sorrento in a villa shared with the Storys.[1]

The exact location of the scene depicted in *Naples* is unknown; but judging from the position of Mount Vesuvius, seen smouldering in the distance, the site must be on the western side of the Bay of Naples near Sorrento. The time is late afternoon. A darkening sky indicates an approaching storm. The low sun delineates foreground details of stones and plants on the steep embankment below the bridge and mellows into haziness over the bay and mountains. The atmospheric lighting, smoking volcano, picturesque crumbling bridge, people in native garb, and quaint house with its lantern and flower pots create a nostalgic picture of rural Italian life.

A painting entitled *Road Scene* was exhibited at the American Art-Union in 1850 (no. 135). It was described in the catalog as "An Italian road scene, with an old bridge in the foreground." The dimensions (twenty-eight by forty-four inches) and description suggest that *Road Scene* is the painting now known as *Naples*.

1. Henry T. Tuckerman, *Book of the Artists* (New York: S. P. Putnam and Sons, 1870), p. 535.

7. Tree Study, *1848*

Oil on board, 10 x 9½ in.
Signed and dated at lower left: J. F. Cropsey/Rome/1848

EX COLLECTIONS
with Jeffrey Alan Gallery, New York.
with Richard Weimer Gallery, Darien, Conn., sold in 1984 to NCF.

This beautifully executed sketch was painted by Jasper Cropsey in Rome in 1848. It displays the variety and deftness of his brushwork and reflects his interest in the play of light on different textures and colors. Cropsey's nature studies are usually focused on a single detail or a small group of natural objects. In *Tree Study*, he highlights one tree in a grove and generalizes the rest of the composition. The low vantage point of the sketch emphasizes the strength and character of the trees. Thick paint adds to their impression of solidity. As in *Solitude* (cat. no. 3), Cropsey uses varying brushstrokes to capture the different textures of bark, foliage, grasses, and earth, giving the surface of the picture an animation that is sometimes lacking in his formal compositions.

 Tree Study is one of a large group of studies of plants and trees that Cropsey painted in Italy. Two others, also done in 1848, are *Study of a Clump of Trees* and *Plants Against Tree Trunk* (both, Museum of Fine Arts, Boston). Most of the surviving studies from Cropsey's stay in Italy were executed not in oil but in pencil and wash.

8. Kneeling Pilgrim, *1849*

Oil on canvas, 13½ x 10 in., arched top
Signed and dated at lower left: J. F. C./Rome/1849

REFERENCE
William S. Talbot, *Jasper F. Cropsey, 1823–1900*, Ph.D. diss., Institute of Fine Arts, New York University,
1972; published New York: Garland Publishing, 1977, no. 43, fig. 37, p. 65.

EX COLLECTIONS
with Kennedy Galleries, New York, 1967.
with Borghe Gallery, New York.
with Richard Weimer Gallery, Darien, Conn., sold in 1984 to NCF.

9. Pilgrim, *1849*

Oil on board, 12½ x 9¾ in.
Signed and dated at lower left: J. F. C./Rome/1849

EX COLLECTIONS
with Skinner Gallery, Boston.
with Richard Weimer Gallery, Darien, Conn., sold in 1984 to NCF.

These two oil studies, painted in Rome in 1849, represent the same pilgrim—an ascetic old man with thinning white hair and a long white beard. He wears a dark robe and carries a staff. The white scallop shell on his chest indicates that he is on a pilgrimage. In each study, the figure occupies an otherwise empty space, with only the vague indication of a ground line. The setting in *Kneeling Pilgrim* is out of doors, with flowers and grasses at the lower edge of the canvas. The figure rests on one knee and appears to have just stopped to pray before a roadside shrine. In *Pilgrim* (p. 48) the figure kneels fully and seems to have been praying for some time, his head deeply bowed.

The pilgrims are quite small in stature, and their bodies are almost completely masked by their robes. Therefore, Cropsey had only to concentrate on the heads and hands. Although during most of his career he participated in life classes at the National Academy, Cropsey rarely included human figures in his paintings except as secondary elements in landscapes. A letter written by his friend John M. Falconer suggests that Cropsey refine his technique in depicting the human form.[1] These studies may have been efforts to improve his skills.[2]

A similar kneeling pilgrim or monk appears in two other paintings made by Cropsey in Italy. They are *Landscape with Figures near Rome*, 1847 (Pennsylvania Academy of the Fine Arts, Philadelphia), and

Kneeling Pilgrim

Pilgrim

Engraved illustration for "The Coliseum," *The Poetical Works of Edgar Allan Poe* (New York: J. S. Redfield, 1858), p. 13.

Three Cypresses, undated (NCF). Cropsey was a pious man who was probably intrigued by the many religious orders that could be found in and around the Vatican. Pilgrims also appear in Cropsey's works after his return from Europe in 1849. In 1850, he participated, with other artists, in painting a series of sixteen scenes from John Bunyan's *Pilgrim's Progress*. For this project, Cropsey painted *Land of Beulah*, 1850 (now unlocated), which depicts the idyllic land reached by the hero at the end of his trials. In 1855, Cropsey proposed to make for his patron Fletcher Williams a series called Pilgrim of the Cross, composed of five paintings that would have traced the journey of the pilgrim through treachery and temptation to the Celestial City.[3] This series is not known to have been executed. Pilgrim figures appear also in Cropsey's illustrations for *The Poetical Works of Edgar Allan Poe* (New York, 1858). For example, the illustration (above) for the poem "The Coliseum" has a kneeling pilgrim similar in conception to *Pilgrim*, 1849.

1. J. Falconer to J. Cropsey, Oct. 29, 1848, Cropsey Papers, NCF, microfilm, roll 336, Arch. Am. Art.
2. Talbot (1972), p. 65.
3. J. Cropsey to F. Williams, Oct. 29, 1855, Cropsey Papers, NCF, microfilm, roll 336, Arch. Am. Art.

10. Rock Study, *1850*

Oil on canvas, 14½ x 9¾ in.
Signed and dated at lower left: J. F. Cropsey/1850

EX COLLECTION
with Richard Weimer Gallery, Darien, Conn., sold in 1985 to NCF.

Jasper Cropsey delighted in the variable contours and complex textures of rock formations. Geological elements are often included in his finished compositions. In *Rock Study*, he captured the intricate textures of the surfaces and the glimmering highlights and subtle shadows cast by the late afternoon sun. Thick, boldly applied paint gives substance and weight to the stones and contrasts with the delicate handling of the flowers and grasses around the outcropping. Frequently, Cropsey placed rocks in the foregrounds of his landscapes to establish the space of the picture and direct the viewer's gaze toward the center of the composition. In *Rock Study*, he concentrated directly on the foreground elements and only hinted at the landscape beyond.

Cropsey's pencil drawings of rocks demonstrate the same sensitive touch and penchant for rendering nuances of light and shadow. In *Boulders Lying in a Field*, 1848 (NCF), he depicts the varying shapes and surface qualities of scattered rocks. The most dramatic of Cropsey's rock studies were executed on a trip to the Dorset coast at Lulworth during his second stay in England. *Cliff, West Lulworth*, 1857 (Museum of Fine Arts, Boston), shows great delicacy of line and precision in recording the crevices and cracks of the dramatic rock formations on the coast.

11. Castle Garden, New York City, *1851*

Oil on canvas, 10½ x 16⅜ in.
Signed and dated at lower right: J. F. Cropsey/1851
On reverse in ink in artist's hand: A sketch of Castle Garden/
for M. Jenny Lind/with the best wishes of the artist/J. F. Cropsey
Collection of The New-York Historical Society

REFERENCE
William S. Talbot, *Jasper F. Cropsey, 1823–1900* (Ph.D. diss., Institute of Fine Arts, New York
University, 1972; New York: Garland Publishing, 1977), pp. 98–99, 362–63.

EX COLLECTIONS
Jenny Lind, 1851.
with Christie's, London, sold on August 1, 1935, no. 128, to Cooling Galleries, London.
with Maurice Sternberg Galleries, Chicago, sold in 1977 to NYHS.

Jasper Cropsey painted *Castle Garden, New York City*, 1851, as a gift for the "Swedish Nightingale," Jenny Lind, who made her American debut at Castle Garden on September 11, 1850. After Cropsey heard her sing there in the spring of 1851, he decided to paint a picture of the location "for the express purpose of presenting it to her as a souvenir of her principal place of song, and of her visit to our country as well as my regard for the fame and virtues she had brought with her and sustained among us." On June 5, 1851, Miss Lind called on Cropsey in his studio to thank him for the gift and told him that it had "touched her heart."[1]

In *Castle Garden, New York City*, 1851, the view is similar to that from Pier 1 on the Hudson River, from which, as Cropsey wrote, "the whole of the Castle—and the Islands in the bay, the lighthouse, and Staten Island come in to the best advantage for a one view observation."[2] Two drawings of Castle Garden, dated May 10 and May 19, 1851, are in the Newington-Cropsey Foundation's collection and were probably made in preparation for this painting. Abraham M. Cozzens commissioned a copy of *Castle Garden, New York City* in June of 1851. That copy is possibly the painting now in the Newington-Cropsey Foundation's collection.

See also *Castle Garden, New York City*, 1859 (cat. no. 27).

1. Jasper F. Cropsey, "A Visit from Jenny Lind," undated MS, coll. Brown Reinhardt, Newark, Del., typescript, pp. 2, 4, NCF.
2. Ibid., p. 1.

12. Skunk Cabbage, *1851*

Oil on academy board, mounted on canvas, 8⅙ x 11½ in.
Signed and dated at lower right: J. F. Cropsey/1851

REFERENCES
Cleveland Museum of Art, Munson-Williams-Proctor Institute, Utica, N.Y., and National Collection
of Fine Arts, Smithsonian Institution, Washington, traveling exhib., 1970–71,
Jasper F. Cropsey, 1823–1900, cat. by William S. Talbot, no. 16, p. 72.
Whitney Museum of American Art, New York, *Reflections of Nature: Flowers in American Art*,
1984, exhib. cat. by Ella M. Foshay, fig. 98, p. 125.

EX COLLECTIONS
Ferdinand H. Davis, New York.
with Richard Weimer Gallery, Darien, Conn., sold in 1983 to NCF.

This small oil painting is a fine example of Cropsey's skill in making botanical studies. He precisely describes the leaves and veins of the skunk cabbage and its thick, fibrous texture. The plant is seen from ground level, and he captures the raking light that falls over and under it from the right-hand side of the picture. The study is painted in smooth, flowing brushstrokes; and the earthy greens of the plant are complemented by touches of bright reds, pinks, and yellows in the small flowers surrounding it. Another oil study executed in 1851, *Hellebore, Iris, and Clover* (coll. Mr. & Mrs. Ferdinand H. Davis, New York), resembles *Skunk Cabbage* in the depiction of light on the plant and the close observation of texture and detail. According to Cropsey:

> The converse with something to give the mind healthy, vigorous powers, is Nature studied as she is, imitated as we see her. This mode of study is productive to knowledge—it makes a man a botanist, a geologist, he is not satisfied in seeing things merely upon the surface. He studies deeper. The knowledge he gains is communicated to his courses, so that while it possesses beauty as a work of art, it is scientific and historical. . . . The mind being thoroughly educated from this close observation of parts and an undeviating resemblance to nature, gives him power to make judicious selections, such, in the view of his exalted mind, as will need no improvements.[1]

Although it is difficult to point to a specific painting for which *Skunk Cabbage* may have been a preliminary study, such plants are frequently included in Cropsey's finished paintings. For example, in *Cottage on Upper Greenwood Lake* (cat. no. 4), a similar plant appears at the lower right.

1. J. Cropsey, "Some Reflections on Natural Art: An Address for the New York Art Re-Union," (Gaylords Bridge, Conn., August 24, 1845), MS, coll. Brown Reinhardt, Newark, Del., typescript, p. 9, NCF.

13. Days of Elizabeth, *1853*

Oil on canvas, 38 x 54 in.
Signed and dated at lower right: J. F. C./1853

REFERENCES

Cleveland Museum of Art, Munson-Williams-Proctor Institute, Utica, N.Y., and National Collection of Fine Arts,
Smithsonian Institution, Washington, traveling exhib., 1970–71, *Jasper F. Cropsey, 1823–1900*, cat. by
William S. Talbot, fig. 7, p. 28, as *Hawking Party in the Time of Queen Elizabeth*.
William S. Talbot, "An Oil Sketch by Jasper Cropsey," *Register of the Museum of Art* 4, no. 1 (1968), fig. b,
pp. 17–22, as *Hawking Party in the Time of Queen Elizabeth*.
William S. Talbot, *Jasper F. Cropsey, 1823–1900*, Ph.D. diss., Institute of Fine Arts, New York University,
1972; published New York: Garland Publishing, 1977, no. 70, fig. 79, p. 111, as *Hawking Party in
the Time of Queen Elizabeth*.
J. Millard Tawes Fine Arts Center, University of Maryland Art Gallery, College Park, *Jasper F. Cropsey, 1823–1900:
A Retrospective View of America's Painter of Autumn*, 1968, exhib. cat. by Peter Bermingham, no. 5, fig. 3, p. 15.

EX COLLECTIONS

E. P. Mitchell, Philadelphia, 1854.
with Berry-Hill Galleries, New York, sold in 1959 to Mr. William Steinschneider, to NCF.

14. Oil Sketch for Days of Elizabeth, *1853*

Oil on canvas, 9 x 14 in.
Signed and dated at lower left: J. F. Cropsey/1853

EX COLLECTION

with Richard Weimer Gallery, Darien, Conn., sold in 1984 to NCF.

Between his two trips to Europe, in 1849 and 1856, Jasper Cropsey painted a number of allegorical and literary subjects. *Days of Elizabeth* was done in 1853 and sold in early 1854 to E. P. Mitchell of Philadelphia. The painting shows a turreted castle and an arched stone bridge set in a vast landscape. In the broad foreground, a hawking party rides out for a day of sport, accompanied by hounds and a man who carries additional birds. The painting is filled with bright sunshine, which highlights the hunters as well as the castle. The figures are very small and consequently appear secondary to the architectural elements in the painting. The prominence of the castle demonstrates Cropsey's professional interest in buildings and his response to the romance of English history.

In *Days of Elizabeth*, Cropsey has represented various aspects of sixteenth-century life. There are victorious soldiers returning from battle, courtiers in the castle garden, hunters, and pastoral figures like the shepherd resting under a tree. No specific story is represented. The different groups of figures

---

56

Days of Elizabeth

engage in separate activities, apart from the other events taking place around them. While the army is greeted by waving spectators in the battlements, for example, archers, beautifully dressed ladies, lovers, an artist and his model, and a robed and turbaned man pursue their own interests, undisturbed.

The oil sketch, one of two known to have been made by Cropsey for *Days of Elizabeth*,[1] does not contain all the figures of the finished painting and is much more compact. The foreground is compressed, and the small scale of the figures is proportional to the landscape. In both the sketch and the finished painting, the sky has been carefully studied. A burst of light through the clouds suggests that a storm is either breaking up or approaching. In the sketch, however, the sky is more brilliantly colored than in the finished picture. The paint is handled loosely in the sketch; and details, save those of the castle, are generalized.

Cropsey's image of courtly life may well have come from reading such writers as Sir Walter Scott, whose poems are filled with episodes involving knights and ladies and chivalric battles. No doubt the literary subjects painted by Thomas Cole also served as a source of inspiration—for example, *Departure* and *Return from the Tournament* (both, 1837, Corcoran Gallery of Art, Washington) and the tournament scene in *Past*, 1838 (Amherst College, Mass.).[2] In all three, there are castles and riders on horseback in landscape settings. *Return from the Tournament* and *Past* have arched stone bridges and distant mountains similar to those in Cropsey's *Days of Elizabeth*. Furthermore, the trees in the left and right foreground of Cropsey's picture are almost identical to those in Cole's *Return from the Tournament*. Nevertheless, while Cropsey may have borrowed the setting and composition from Cole, he selected the specific subject for *Days of Elizabeth* and the details himself.

1. The other sketch for *Days of Elizabeth*, also dated 1853, is in the Spencer Museum of Art, University of Kansas, Lawrence. It is slightly smaller in size.
2. Talbot (1968), pp. 21–22.

Oil Sketch for Days of Elizabeth

15. Niagara, *1853*

Oil on canvas, 48 x 72 in.
Signed and dated at lower right: J. F. Cropsey/1853

REFERENCE
Albright-Knox Art Gallery, Buffalo, N.Y., Corcoran Gallery of Art, Washington, The New-York
Historical Society, traveling exhib., 1985–86, *Niagara: Two Centuries of Changing Attitudes,
1697–1901*, cat. by Jeremy E. Adamson with essays by Elizabeth McKinsey, Alfred
Runte, and John F. Sears, no. 55, fig. 42, pp. 52–53.

EX COLLECTIONS
probably a Major Cabney (sale, held in artist's studio, April 1856).
with Mrs. Donald Webster, Chevy Chase, Md.
with Weiman and Weiman, Woodbridge, Conn., sold in 1981 to NCF.

In August of 1852, during a sketching trip through New York, Vermont, and New Hampshire, Jasper Cropsey made his first visit to Niagara Falls, where he stayed for about a week. While there, he completed "four studies in oil [and] two passably good pencil drawings." For these works, he gave his specific vantage point as a small island below the cataracts, from which the two great falls, American and Central (or Crescent), could be seen to best advantage. Cropsey had to wade to the island until he "employed some boys to lay stepping stones."[1] Peter Porter, a local real estate agent, had pointed out the spot; and Cropsey later noted that the view from this position had never been painted.[2] Working conditions were difficult. He complained that mist and water kept ruining his canvases.[3]

Niagara must have been produced from one of the four oil studies that Cropsey made during this trip. The emphasis is on the American Falls, the partially visible Cave of the Winds, and the rocks on the right. In the distance, high on the Canadian side, there is a glimpse of Clifton House, overlooking the falls. The atmospheric effects—spray, heavy mist, and a rainbow shimmering in the vapor along the base of the falls—are dramatic. The painting is full of movement from the energetic brushwork and the brilliant play of light over the rough waters.

Enthusiastic letters to his wife, Maria, describe Cropsey's days at Niagara, including two days working side by side with John F. Kensett. In *Niagara Falls*, 1853–54 (White House Collection, Washington), Kensett shows the falls at a great distance, placed undramatically within a broad, horizontal composition. Contrastingly, Cropsey's view is charged with excitement. It conveys the power and drama of the falling water by the unusually close viewpoint. Both Kensett and Cropsey emphasized the choppy water of the river and its large, jagged boulders. Frederick E. Church also worked at Niagara in the 1850s. His most notable painting of the falls is *Niagara*, 1857 (Corcoran Gallery of Art, Washington). Like Cropsey, Church chose a scintillating viewpoint: the river above the falls with the water thundering over the cliff in a sweeping semi-circle.

There were two instances in 1853 of the exhibition of a Cropsey painting entitled *Niagara*. One was at the National Academy of Design's annual exhibition (no. 23); and the other, in December at the American Art-Union. Probably in both cases the painting was the same. The recorded dimensions coincide with the painting shown here. In the 1856 sale of Cropsey's works, prior to his departure for England, a large painting entitled *Niagara* was purchased by a Major Cabney.[1]

1. J. Cropsey to his wife, Maria, August 22 and August 16, 1852, coll. Brown Reinhardt, Newark, Del., typescript, NCF.
2. J. Cropsey to John W. Kitchell, Nov. 1, 1897, John W. Kitchell Papers, microfilm, roll 1356, Arch. Am. Art.
3. J. Cropsey to M. Cropsey, August 16, 1852, coll. Brown Reinhardt, Newark, Del., typescript, NCF.
4. List of paintings in 1856 sale, published in *Hagadorn's Semi-Weekly Staaten Islander* (April 12, 1856), p. 2.

16. Days of Chivalry, *1854*

Oil on canvas, 8¾ x 13¾ in.
Signed and dated at lower right: J. F. Cropsey/1854

Days of Chivalry might be more appropriately titled *Return from Hawking*. In this oil sketch, Cropsey paints a landscape with a castle in the background and a group of three mounted figures with their attendants in the right foreground. Before them trudges a man carrying the spoils of the hunt.

Days of Chivalry is similar to Cropsey's sketch (cat. no. 14) for *Days of Elizabeth*, 1853. The two studies were painted within about six months of one another. In both, trees frame an open field in the foreground and a stream flows along the edge of the clearing and under an arched stone bridge. The hunting parties are at the right in both compositions, and a castle looms above each scene—although on opposite sides of the paintings. These similarities in composition and the fact that the dimensions of the two sketches are identical suggest that Cropsey modeled *Days of Chivalry* on the earlier painting.

In 1854, a painting entitled *Return from Hawking* (now unlocated) was sold by Cropsey to James L. Claghorn of Philadelphia along with another painting.[1] Tuckerman also lists *Return from Hawking* as being in Claghorn's collection.[2] A picture of the same title, nineteen by twenty-nine inches, was in the James L. Claghorn sale in 1877.[3] Perhaps *Days of Chivalry* was a preliminary study for this larger painting.

1. Cropsey's account book, 1854, Cropsey Papers, NCF, microfilm, roll 336, Arch. Am. Art.
2. *Book of the Artists* (New York: G. P. Putnam & Son, 1867), p. 538.
3. James L. Claghorn sale, Somerville auctioneer, Philadelphia, April 18 and 19, 1877, no. 60. See William S. Talbot, *Jasper F. Cropsey, 1823–1900* (Ph.D. diss., Institute of Fine Arts, New York University, 1972; published New York: Garland Publishing, 1977), p. 372.

17. The Millennial Age, *1854*

Oil on canvas, 38 x 54 in.
Signed and dated at lower right: J. F. Cropsey/1854

REFERENCES
Cleveland Museum of Art, Munson-Williams-Proctor Institute, Utica, N.Y., and National Collection
of Fine Arts, Smithsonian Institution, Washington, traveling exhib., 1970–71,
Jasper F. Cropsey, 1823–1900, cat. by William S. Talbot, no. 19, ill., pp. 73, 76.
William S. Talbot, *Jasper F. Cropsey, 1823–1900*, Ph.D. diss., Institute of Fine Arts, New York University,
1972; published New York: Garland Publishing, 1977, no. 75, fig. 81, pp. 112–13,
375–76.
J. Millard Tawes Fine Arts Center, University of Maryland Art Gallery, College Park,
Jasper F. Cropsey, 1823–1900: A Retrospective View of America's Painter of Autumn, 1968, exhib. cat.
by Peter Bermingham, no. 6, fig. 2, p. 15.

EX COLLECTIONS
E. P. Mitchell, Philadelphia, 1854 or 1855.
probably Joseph Harrison, Philadelphia.
Charles Knox Smith, possibly Philadelphia.
with Kennedy Galleries, New York, sold in 1965 to Mr. and Mrs. John C. Newington.

Jasper Cropsey's interest in allegorical and religious subjects found full expression in his 1854 painting *The Millennial Age*. It represents a new age of peace and prosperity in which the arts flourish and man's relationship with nature is renewed. The setting is a magnificent Mediterranean landscape with the sea shimmering in the background. The focal point of the painting is a huge sculpture surmounted by a lion, a child, a lamb, and a calf. The square stone slab on which they rest is supported by a band of maidens in classical drapery. There are two *putti*—one carrying a cross and the other holding a banner that reads, "On Earth Peace." An open Bible at the base of the monument is inscribed "Isaiah II:4" and "Isaiah XI:6." These Biblical passages foretell the coming of Christ's kingdom when there will be no more war and all living beings will exist in harmony with one another. Cropsey made a preliminary design for the sculpture in *The Millennial Age* (drawing, ca. 1854, NCF; see p. 23) but altered it in the painting.

The Millennial Age is strongly reminiscent of the works of Thomas Cole. During Cropsey's lifetime, his work was frequently compared to Cole's, and Cropsey was himself a great admirer of the older artist. *The Millennial Age* recalls Cole's *The Pastoral State*, undated (NYHS), from his Course of Empire series, as well as *The Dream of Arcadia*, 1838 (Denver Art Museum). In *The Pastoral State*, figures pursue such activities as mathematics, music, dance, and agriculture in a beautiful, open landscape enhanced by an air of peace and prosperity. *The Dream of Arcadia* is a similar, peaceful, pastoral scene. In both, the figures live in accord with nature; but their lives are also governed by religion, symbolized in each painting by a temple.

Cropsey based *The Millennial Age* on his earlier painting entitled *The Spirit of Peace*, 1851 (Woodmere Art Museum, Philadelphia; see p. 25). While some elements have been altered or eliminated in the later work, both paintings feature a Mediterranean setting and describe an age of concord and bounty. In 1854 or 1855, *The Millennial Age* was purchased by one of Cropsey's patrons, E. P. Mitchell, who also owned *Days of Elizabeth* (cat. no. 13). By 1856, Joseph Harrison of Philadelphia had acquired a painting entitled *The Millennial Age*, which seems likely to have been this one.

18. Autumn, *1855*

Oil on canvas, 18 in. diameter
Signed and dated at lower left: J. F. Cropsey/1855

REFERENCES
Cleveland Museum of Art, Munson-Williams-Proctor Institute, Utica, N.Y., and National Collection
of Fine Arts, Smithsonian Institution, Washington, traveling exhib., 1970–71,
Jasper F. Cropsey, 1823–1900, cat. by William S. Talbot, no. 21, p. 78.
William S. Talbot, *Jasper F. Cropsey, 1823–1900*, Ph.D. diss., Institute of Fine Arts, New York University,
1972; published New York: Garland Publishing, 1977, no. 90, fig. 62, pp. 97–98.
J. Millard Tawes Fine Arts Center, University of Maryland Art Gallery, College Park,
Jasper F. Cropsey, 1823–1900: A Retrospective View of America's Painter of Autumn, 1968, exhib.
cat. by Peter Bermingham, no. 3, fig. 7, p. 19.

EX COLLECTIONS
possibly a Dr. Crane, New York.
with Victor D. Spark, New York, sold in 1967 to Mr. and Mrs. John C. Newington.

19. Summer, *1855*

Oil on canvas, 18 in. diameter
Signed and dated at lower right: J. F. Cropsey/1855

REFERENCES
Talbot (1972), no. 91, fig. 63, pp. 97–98.
University of Maryland (1968), no. 4, fig. 8.

EX COLLECTIONS
possibly a Dr. Crane, New York.
with Victor D. Spark, New York, sold in 1967 to Mr. and Mrs. John C. Newington.

These two circular paintings are presumably part of a series, of which the other two paintings are unlocated. In *Autumn* and *Summer*, Cropsey has employed a similar format: a body of water in the foreground, woodlands in the middle ground, and a pointed mountain peak in the background. The contour of the mountain range suggests that the location might be the same in both panels, only seen from a closer viewpoint in *Autumn*. In fact, judging from other landscapes that Cropsey painted around 1855—for example, *Autumn—Chocorua Peak, White Mountains*, 1856 (private collection, New Hope, Pa.)— the location may be in the White Mountains in New Hampshire; and the peak, Mount Chocorua, which Cropsey depicted frequently in the 1850s. In late summer and early autumn of 1855, Cropsey made a sketching trip to Niagara Falls and the White Mountains. Therefore, White Mountain scenery would have been fresh in his mind.[1]

Autumn

Autumn, with its dramatic, cloud-filled sky and dead tree trunks, is reminiscent of works by Thomas Cole, such as *Landscape with Tree Trunks*, 1827–28 (Rhode Island School of Design, Providence). The composition includes a blasted tree in the foreground, a storm brewing over a lake, and distant mountains seen through mist and clouds. Both Cole and Cropsey found autumn coloring and atmospheric effects most effectively expressed in a rugged mountain landscape.

Summer has a softer and more cultivated landscape. A young woman, holding a lunch basket and wearing a broad-brimmed hat, sits quietly by the water, enjoying the pleasures of a warm, summer day. In the distance, below the tall peak, a small farm is visible. Cropsey's vision of summer is a pastoral landscape where man is in harmony with nature. It is very different in effect as well as coloring from the wilder landscape of *Autumn*.

In his account book for 1855 and 1858, Cropsey recorded that he sold three paintings to a Dr. Crane: "Autumn, one of the series," on May 20, 1855, and *Spring* and *Winter*, both eighteen inches in diameter, on August 12, 1858.[2] These records suggest that Dr. Crane probably bought a full cycle of round season paintings, although no panel for summer is documented. Perhaps the paintings *Summer* and *Autumn* shown here were among those purchased by Dr. Crane.

1. J. Cropsey to his wife, Maria, Sept. 2, 1855, coll. Brown Reinhardt, Newark, Del., typescript, NCF.
2. Cropsey's account book, 1845–1868, Cropsey Papers, NCF, microfilm, roll 336, Arch. Am. Art.

Summer

20. Capri—Moonlight, *1855*

Oil on canvas, 27½ x 41 in.
Signed and dated at lower right: J. F. Cropsey/1855

REFERENCE
William S. Talbot, *Jasper F. Cropsey, 1823–1900*, Ph.D. diss., Institute of Fine Arts, New York University,
1972; published New York: Garland Publishing, 1977, no. 77, fig. 74, pp. 104, 377.

EX COLLECTION
J. Cooper Lord, New York, 1855.

During the 1850s, Jasper Cropsey painted a number of scenes that were inspired by his visit to Italy from 1847 to 1849. *Capri—Moonlight* and two other paintings from that period, *Morning, Coast of Sicily*, 1855, and *Evening at Paestum*, 1856 (both, Vassar College Art Gallery, Poughkeepsie, N.Y.), show his increasing interest in capturing specific times of day and seasonal effects.

In *Capri—Moonlight* the sun sets over the water as a full moon rises. The sky is rendered in vibrant sunset reds and oranges, stormy grays, and pale moonlight. Big, billowy clouds contrast with storm clouds. The empty shore and a ruined tower convey a quiet, lonely mood. The tower, standing at the upper end of the beach, is similar to the ruin in Thomas Cole's painting *The Present*, 1838 (Amherst College, Mass.). The glistening sea, fragments of fallen architecture, and dramatic sky give *Capri—Moonlight* an evocative and dreamlike effect. Perhaps fond memories of Italy and his anticipation of another trip to Europe in 1856 elicited from Cropsey this romantic vision of the Italian seacoast.

J. Cooper Lord bought the painting in February of 1855[1] and showed it that year at the National Academy of Design's annual exhibition, as *Mediterranean Sea Coast* (no. 21). A review called the painting "a daring success," said the scene was "rendered by a master, in a poetical and feeling manner," and mentioned the effect of blended sunlight and moonlight.[2]

1. Cropsey's account book, 1855, Cropsey Papers, NCF, microfilm, roll 336, Arch. Am. Art.
2. "Exhibition of the National Academy of Design," *Knickerbocker* 45 (May 1855), p. 532.

21. The Good Shepherd, *1855*

Oil on canvas, 28½ x 44½ in.
Signed and dated at lower center: J. F. Cropsey/1855

The Good Shepherd serves as an example of Jasper Cropsey's interest in religious and allegorical painting during the mid-1850s. Within its beautiful rolling landscape, Christ stands beside a lake, staff in hand, tending his flock of sheep. The sheep are marked with red crosses on their backs, perhaps alluding to the sacrifice of Christ. Other symbols that convey the idea of Christ as savior are the Easter lilies that grow in the foreground, reminding the viewer of Christ's resurrection. The pristine landscape reinforces the redemptive values implicit in the figure of Christ. The bright, clear sky, still waters, and verdant, gently sloping hills represent the new Eden assured by Christ to the faithful.

The Good Shepherd was purchased by Fletcher Williams in May of 1855 and impressed him enough to commission Cropsey later the same year to design a series of paintings "of a religious kind, something in the vein of Cole."[1] A series called Pilgrim of the Cross was proposed by Cropsey in October of 1855, but it is not known to have been executed. Cropsey described Williams as a man whose "love for pictures is of a purely religious kind."[2]

Cropsey saw *The Good Shepherd* in Williams's home in August of 1855 and varnished it there. He wrote to Maria that his patron was very pleased with the painting but that it was badly lit.[3]

1. J. Cropsey to his wife, Maria, Sept. 2, 1855, coll. Brown Reinhardt, Newark, Del., typescript, NCF.
2. J. Cropsey to F. Williams, Oct. 29, 1855, Cropsey Papers, NCF, microfilm, roll 336, Arch. Am. Art.
3. J. Cropsey to M. Cropsey, August 31, 1855, coll. Brown Reinhardt, typescript, NCF.

22. Tree Study, *1855*

Oil on paper, mounted on canvas 15¾ x 11 in.
Signed and dated at lower left: J. F. C./1855

EX COLLECTIONS
with George Subkoff Gallery, New York.
with Richard Weimer Gallery, Darien, Conn., sold in 1985 to NCF.

In the foregrounds of his landscape paintings, Cropsey frequently used old, craggy trees like the one in this study. The gnarled trunks and convoluted branches offered interesting variations of color, texture, and line. Furthermore, these weather-beaten, timeworn trees could introduce a sense of history into a painting. They had long been used in landscape paintings to indicate the passage of time and its effect on nature. They were prominent, for example, in the work of Thomas Cole, whom Cropsey greatly admired.

Tree Study shows only the trunk and lower branches of the tree. It appears to be almost dead. Only a few leaves along the upper edge of the picture suggest that the tree still has some life. In contrast, alongside the aged tree is an upright, leafy sapling that has not yet suffered the abuses of weather and time. Together they embody Cropsey's belief that "Nature, in all ages and in all periods of her existence, . . . has possessed undiminished her beauty and I may add, the same power over the mind."[1]

1. J. F. Cropsey, "Some Reflections on Natural Art: An Address for the New York Art Re-Union" (Gaylords Bridge, Conn., August 24, 1845), MS, coll. Brown Reinhardt, Newark, Del., typescript, p. 1, NCF.

23. Chenango River, New York, *1856*

Oil on canvas, 25⅜ x 40¾ in.
Signed and dated at lower left: J. F. Cropsey/1856

Chenango River, New York was painted just before Cropsey's second trip to England in 1856. It depicts a peaceful afternoon along the banks of the Chenango River, where cows graze and farmhands work in the fields outside a small village. Only church steeples, a bridge, and several small houses are visible within the burgeoning landscape. The picture is dominated by a cloud-streaked sky. Fluffy white clouds float above the mountains, while a storm cloud intrudes at the left. In a letter written during a trip to Chenango County, Cropsey expressed his fondness for the area. "The scenery is very beautiful," he wrote, "full of beautiful trees and I think looks like the Land of Beulah only I don't quite see the figures with shining wings."[1]

Chenango River, New York was shown at the annual exhibition of the National Academy of Design in 1856 as *Chenango River Scenery* (no. 148). Critics ordinarily praised the work that Cropsey produced prior to his departure for England, but this painting received mixed reviews.[2] The critic for the *New York Evening Post* wrote that it "has good distance, a good feeling for effect, a pleasing composition, and has some bits of exquisite painting, as in the house and bridge, but it is marred by carelessness and deficiency of study, unworthy of an artist of first-rate standing."[3] "Deficiency of study" referred to Cropsey's rendering of the cows in the river, criticized also by a writer for the *Crayon*, who commented, "Did Mr. Cropsey never observe that cattle, in descending a slope, plant the hind feet so far forward, that the back preserves its level? And could he not see, that several of his herd must inevitably fall on their heads?"[4] However, the same critic praised Cropsey's "excellent taste in the matter of foregrounds." The rendering of livestock in such later paintings as *Cows on River*, 1887 (cat. no. 45), shows that Cropsey had worked to overcome his earlier deficiencies.

1. J. Cropsey to his wife, Maria, August 29, 1852, coll. Brown Reinhardt, Newark, Del., typescript, NCF.
2. "The Fine Arts. Exhibition at the National Academy," *Literary World* 1 (May 8, 1847), p. 323.
3. "National Academy—No. 4," *New York Evening Post* (April 21, 1856), p. 2.
4. "Exhibition of the National Academy of Design," *Crayon* 3 (April 1856), p. 117.

24. Springtime on the Hudson, *1856*

Oil on canvas, 31½ x 18½ in.
Signed and dated at lower left: J. F. Cropsey/1856

EX COLLECTION
with Richard Weimer Gallery, Darien, Conn., sold in 1985 to NCF.

In the mid-1850s, Jasper Cropsey began to paint seasonal pictures with greater frequency. Although heralded today for his autumn scenes, he painted the other seasons as well. *Springtime on the Hudson* is brimming with lush foliage and flowers. Workers are busy bailing hay, while cows graze in the fields and wade in the stream. The Hudson River separates the foreground from hills and a small town in the distance. The view is framed by large, spreading trees with dark green leaves that contrast with the bright sky. The viewer is invited into this charming landscape by the footpath at the lower left.

This quiet, rural scene was modeled on a small oil study by the same title, 1855 (NCF). *Springtime on the Hudson* and *Chenango River, New York* (cat. no. 23), both painted in 1856, are quite similar, especially in the attention lavished on the sky. In "Up among the Clouds," Cropsey discussed the necessity of a truthful rendering of the sky. He described three types of clouds—cirrus, cumulus, and nimbus—and the expressive qualities inherent in each. The cirrus and cumulus clouds are usually associated with "soothing and poetical thoughts of serenest beauty," whereas the nimbus is capable of "awakening the deepest emotions of gloom, dread, and fear; or sending thrilling sensations of joy and gladness through our being."[1] In *Springtime on the Hudson*, cumulus clouds fill the afternoon sky; while nimbus clouds, foretelling rain, begin to gather.

1. Jasper F. Cropsey, "Up among the Clouds," *Crayon* 2 (August 8, 1855), pp. 79–80.

25. Stateroom on Ship en Route to England, *1856*

Oil on canvas, 11 x 14½ in.
Signed and dated at lower right: J. F. Cropsey/1856

The Cropseys sailed for England aboard the *Devonshire* in early June of 1856. They settled in London and remained there until July 1863, when they returned to the United States. *Stateroom on Ship en Route to England* was painted either during the crossing or soon after their arrival in England. It depicts Cropsey's wife, Maria, reading in the background, and their two daughters, Mary (1850–1921) and Jennie (b. 1852), sewing and having tea in the foreground. Some of the family's belongings—trunks, coats, and hats—can be seen in the bright sunlight that illuminates the cabin.

Stateroom on Ship en Route to England is the only picture thought to have been painted by Cropsey aboard the ship and the only one of his family save an unfinished portrait of Maria that he was painting when he died. Figure studies in general are rare in his work.

26. Study for Starrucca Viaduct—Autumn, *1856*

Oil on canvas, 12 x 18 in.

REFERENCE
Roberson Center for the Arts and Sciences, Binghampton, N.Y., *Susquehanna: Images of the Settled Landscape*, 1981, exhib. cat. by Roger B. Stein, p. 62.

EX COLLECTIONS
estate of the artist.
descended through family to NCF.

As early as October of 1853, Jasper Cropsey made his first studies of this imposing railroad bridge. *Starrucca Vale*, 1853 (Museum of Fine Arts, Boston), a drawing, shows the same view as this painting: the Susquehanna valley with mountains in the distance and a train beginning to cross the viaduct in the middle ground. The Starrucca viaduct, part of the Erie Railroad, was built in 1848 near Lanesboro, Pennsylvania. Acclaimed as one of the finest stone bridges in the country, it was considered an engineering triumph and was a popular stop for travelers.[1]

Concerning the beauty of the Susquehanna valley, Cropsey wrote, "What a beautiful view from the R.R. bridge looking over the Susquehanna, how green and delightful were the meadows—how luxuriant and beautiful were the trees—how white and tidy were the houses and how many wealthy looking cottages among them—how the horses in the meadow did scamper as the train passed their full mane long tail and graceful movements came in very beautiful with the flourishing and suburban appearance of all around." In the same letter, he described the landscape as "Durandish." He must have been very impressed with the countryside, because he returned a year later and wrote, "I find the place beautiful. If I can have good weather I shall get some very fine material here."[2] From this second excursion to the Susquehanna valley, Cropsey produced the drawing *Starrucca Vale*, on which the oil study seems to be modeled.

He has chosen a vantage point above the untouched forest, where he can look out over a cultivated landscape and a village to the train, a contrasting symbol of industrial progress. Neither the train nor the viaduct disrupts the tranquillity and beauty of the scene. The train passes unobtrusively through the landscape, along a track that echoes the curve of the river, and is made noticeable chiefly by the billowing smoke from its locomotive. The arches of the viaduct reflect bright sunshine. The colors are autumnal reds, golds, browns, and oranges, all brushed energetically over the canvas. A threat of rain is implied by the cloudy, darkening sky.

Cropsey completed several large paintings of the Starrucca viaduct in the 1860s, including *Starrucca Viaduct—Autumn*, 1865 (Toledo Museum of Art, Ohio), and the very grand version of the scene entitled *An American Autumn*, probably also painted in 1865, which was the third prize in the 1867 lottery to

benefit the Crosby Opera House in Chicago. Unfortunately, the painting was destroyed in the Chicago fire of 1871. It had, however, been chromolithographed by T. Sinclair of Philadelphia. The reproductions, entitled *American Autumn: Starrucca Valley, Erie Railroad*, were offered as a gift to anyone who purchased at least four shares in the 1867 lottery.

1. Roberson Center (1981), p. 62.
2. J. Cropsey to his wife, Maria, August 5, 1852, and Oct. 13, 1853, coll. Brown Reinhardt, Newark, Del., typescripts, NCF.

27. Castle Garden, New York City, *1859*

Oil on canvas, 15⅛ x 24¼ in.
Signed and dated at lower center: J. F. Cropsey/1859
On wood backing panel in pencil: Castle Garden, New York/J. F. Cropsey—London—1859
Collection of The New-York Historical Society

REFERENCE
William S. Talbot, *Jasper F. Cropsey, 1823–1900*, Ph.D. diss., Institute of Fine Arts, New York
University, 1972; published New York: Garland Publishing, 1977, p. 364.

EX COLLECTIONS
possibly E. Gambert, London, 1859.
Percy R. Pyne II, London (sale, 1917, no. 133, ill., as *Battery by Moonlight*).
private collection, Southampton, N.Y.
Charles Burr Lamar, New York, sold in 1972 to NYHS.

Castle Garden, New York City, 1859, is modeled after an oil sketch of the same year, entitled *Castle Garden* (NCF). Although moonlit scenes, they give the same view as Cropsey's 1851 painting (cat. no. 11). Done while Cropsey was in London, *Castle Garden, New York City*, 1859, may be the same painting that was sold to the lithographer E. Gambert on July 28th of that year, along with three other landscapes.[1]

Castle Garden began as Fort Clinton, completed around 1810 at the Battery in Manhattan. After the War of 1812, the garrison was dismantled; and the fort, then called Castle Clinton, was turned over to the city. In the 1820s, the building, renamed Castle Garden, was converted into a concert hall and entertainment center, "considered at the time to be the largest audience-room in the world."[2] It remained popular for the next twenty-five years. During the second half of the nineteenth century, Castle Garden served as an immigration station. In the 1890s, when the Immigration Commission offices moved to Ellis Island, Castle Garden was made into a public aquarium. Today, once again called Castle Clinton, it is a national monument, administered by the National Park Service.

1. Cropsey's account book, 1859, Cropsey Papers, NCF, microfilm, roll 336, Arch. of Am. Art.
2. William Loring Andrews, *The Iconography of the Battery and Castle Garden* (New York: Charles Scribner's Sons, 1901), p. 32.

28. Temple at Paestum, Crescent Moon, *1859*

Oil on canvas, 31½ x 51½ in.
Signed and dated at lower right: J. F. Cropsey/1859

EX COLLECTION
possibly J. W. Brown, London, August 4, 1859.

Temple at Paestum, Crescent Moon was painted by Cropsey during his second trip to England. It shows the classical temple of Neptune and, in the distance, the archaic temple of Ceres. The painting was exhibited in 1859 at the Royal Academy of Arts, London, as *Paestum* (no. 924). A critic of the London *Art Journal* called it "a scene of imposing solemnity."[1] The *London Times* critic said the painting was "a nobly conceived and solemn reproduction of those gigantic Doric monuments."[2] Both were impressed by the drama and severity of the scene.

Cropsey had visited Paestum on a sketching trip in August of 1848 with the American artists Christopher P. Cranch and William Wetmore Story. Cranch's description of their first sight of Paestum parallels Cropsey's painting: "Our visit to these famous old ruins was on a lovely, breezy day. As we approached them we could none of us resist the most enthusiastic exclamations of delight. Never had I seen anything more perfect, such exquisite proportions, such warm, rich coloring, such picturesquely broken columns; flowers and briers growing in and around, and sometimes over fallen capitals. Right through between the columns gleamed the sea, and beyond, the blue, misty mountains. And over all brooded such a silence and solitude. Nothing stood between us and the Past, to mar the impression. Mysterious, beautiful temples!" After their initial sighting of the temples, Cranch wrote, "we took our repast in the great temple of Neptune; then betook ourselves resolutely to sketching. . . . They told us it was unsafe to remain here after three o'clock on account of the malaria. Our stay was too brief, but the sun began to descend, and we hurried away."[3]

Temple at Paestum, Crescent Moon seems to have been modeled upon an earlier painting by Cropsey entitled *Evening at Paestum*, 1856 (Vassar College Art Gallery, Poughkeepsie, N.Y.). Elias Lyman Magoon bought *Evening at Paestum* in February and a duplicate in November of 1859. The same year, Cropsey sold a painting entitled *Temple at Paestum* to J. W. Brown.[4] This is probably the painting shown here.

1. "The Exhibition of the Royal Academy," *Art Journal* (London) (June 1859), pp. 161–72.
2. "Royal Academy Exhibition. Second Notice," *London Times* (May 10, 1859), p. 4.
3. Quoted in Lenora Cranch Scott, *The Life and Letters of Christopher Pearse Cranch* (Boston: Houghton Mifflin Company, 1917), p. 147.
4. Cropsey's account book, 1856 and 1859, Cropsey Papers, NCF, microfilm, roll 336, Arch. Am. Art.

29. Greenwood Lake, *1862*

Oil on canvas, 33 x 53 in.
Signed and dated at lower right: J. F. Cropsey/1862

EX COLLECTION
with Richard Weimer Gallery, Darien, Conn., sold in 1983 to NCF.

Although representing an American location, *Greenwood Lake* was painted during Jasper Cropsey's second stay in England. A late afternoon scene in autumn, it offers a partial view of the lake with a broad foreground area of the shore and a background of fields and mountains. The still waters, setting sun, and long shadows, together with the rolling landscape, create a mood of tranquillity. Children play on the shore and pick berries in the brambles. Here, as in other works of Cropsey's mid-career, the figures take on greater prominence, probably because he was becoming more skillful in depicting the human figure.

The foreground of *Greenwood Lake* shows Cropsey's expert treatment of details. Every leaf, branch, stone, and blade of grass is delineated with clarity and realism that recall his *Autumn on the Hudson*, 1860 (National Gallery of Art, Washington), which was also painted in England. This pronounced interest in the precise rendering of minute details may have resulted from Cropsey's exposure to Pre-Raphaelite art in England and his friendship with John Ruskin, the champion of the movement. In both paintings the background details are fully formed but made indistinct by a haze that falls over water and land.

Another painting, *Autumn, Greenwood Lake*, 1866 (NCF), is similar in color and treatment to both *Greenwood Lake* and *Autumn on the Hudson*. The use of warm colors and pervasive golden light in all three paintings may reflect the influence of J. M. W. Turner. While Cropsey was in England, his work was likened to Turner's; and certainly these tonal effects are key features of Turner's landscapes.[1] Cropsey would have seen Turner's paintings in London and probably attended the large exhibition of them that was organized by John Ruskin and held at Marlborough House in November 1856.[2]

1. "'Autumn on the Hudson.' The Painting by Mr. Cropsey," *Art Journal* (London) (July 1, 1860), pp. 198–99.
2. William S. Talbot, *Jasper F. Cropsey, 1823–1900* (Ph.D. diss., Institute of Fine Arts, New York University, 1972; published New York: Garland Publishing, 1977), p. 123.

30. Civil War Scenes, *ca. 1863*

Supply Wagon and Guards
Forced Cavalry March with Scouts
Around the Campfire
Under Fire in the Woods
Wading through Stream on Moonlit Night
Union Soldiers on March, Zouaves Regiment
Soldier Courting Girl in Pink Dress
Black Dog Barking at a Laying Hen

Oil on paper, mounted on cardboard, each 2½ x 4 in.

EX COLLECTION
with Weiss Gallery, New York, sold in 1949 to Mr. William Steinschneider, to NCF.

Soon after Jasper Cropsey and his family returned to New York from England in July of 1863, the artist traveled to Gettysburg, Pennsylvania, to witness the aftermath of the Civil War. He must have painted these eight oil sketches at that time. Their small size and rapid execution suggest that they were made on location. The sketches all have a horizontal format and generalized landscape backgrounds. All but one are vignettes of military life and regimental activities. The figures, sometimes grouped in a mass, are unidentifiable. Two of the pictures, *Around the Campfire* and *Wading through Stream on Moonlit Night*, are night scenes in which Cropsey has skillfully captured the glow of firelight in the trees and moonlight on the water. The locations of the eight scenes are unknown.

In 1866, Cropsey exhibited a painting called *Gettysburg* (unlocated) at the National Academy of Design's annual exhibition (no. 409). A printed description of the painting pinpoints the scene as the place where the first day of battle took place, with part of the town of Gettysburg in the distance. Locations of interest, such as the rebel encampment, Lee's headquarters, and McMillan's orchard, are listed as having been included in the painting. The closing lines of the description read, "All of the details were most carefully studied by the artist, on the spot, a few months after the battle took place, and before any important changes were made."[1] Other Civil War paintings by Cropsey are *The Round Top and Headquarters of General Meade at Gettysburg* (exhibited 1867, Pennsylvania Academy of the Fine Arts, Philadelphia, ann. exhib., no. 164) and *Scene at Gettysburg* (sale, Leeds Gallery, New York, 1868),[2] both of which are now unlocated.

The eight small sketches are not preliminary studies for any of the paintings mentioned above; but in all probability, Cropsey made them in anticipation of a similar, large, finished work. Judging

Supply Wagon and Guards

Forced Cavalry March with Scouts

from the attention to topographical and historical details in his large Gettysburg scenes, Cropsey must have relied heavily on written descriptions of the battle and the many annotated maps that were published during and after the Civil War.

1. "Mr. Cropsey's Picture of the Battlefield of Gettysburg," undated, Cropsey Papers, NCF, microfilm, roll 336, Arch. Am. Art.
2. William S. Talbot, *Jasper F. Cropsey, 1823–1900* (Ph.D. diss., Institute of Fine Arts, New York University, 1972; published New York: Garland Publishing, 1977), p. 173.

Around the Campfire

Under Fire in the Woods

Wading through Stream on Moonlit Night

Union Soldiers on March, Zouaves Regiment

Soldier Courting Girl in Pink Dress

Black Dog Barking at a Laying Hen

31. Lake George, *1870*

Oil on canvas, 24 x 43¾ in.
Signed and dated at lower left: J. F. Cropsey/1870

EX COLLECTION
with Hirschl and Adler Galleries, New York, sold in 1972 to Mr. and Mrs. John C. Newington.

At the eastern edge of the Adirondack Mountains, midway between Lake Champlain and Canada, lies Lake George. Its spectacular beauty was widely acclaimed in the nineteenth century and attracted artists such as Asher B. Durand, John F. Kensett, and Jasper F. Cropsey. The first visit by Cropsey may have been as early as 1855. During the 1860s, he painted the lake several times, for example, in *Lake George: Sunrise*, 1868 (IBM Corporation, New York), and *Lake George: Sunset*, 1867 (NYHS, on permanent loan from New York Public Library).

In *Lake George*, 1870, soft light bathes the lake, its many rocks and islands, and the two mountains that slope gracefully to its shore. Cropsey has captured the smooth, reflective surface of the lake, which the Indians called *Horicon*, or "silvery water." In the foreground, the water is so transparent that it reveals the yellow sand on the lake bottom.

The popularity of Lake George as a vacation spot grew from descriptions like this one in a guidebook of Cropsey's time: "It is surrounded by high and picturesque hills, sometimes rising to mountain height, and dotted with numerous islands, said to count as many as there are days in the year; some are of considerable size, and cultivated; while others are only a barren rock, rising majestically out of the surrounding waters. The wild and romantic scenery of the lake is nowhere surpassed."[1]

1. John Disturnell, comp., *The Travelers Guide to the Hudson River, Saratoga Springs, Lake George, Falls of Niagara and Thousand Islands* (New York: American News Company, 1864), p. 197.

32. Lake Scene, Franconia Notch, *1870*

Oil on canvas, 16 x 22 in.
Signed and dated at lower left: J. F. Cropsey/1870

EX COLLECTIONS
with M. R. Schweitzer, New York.
White House Collection, Washington.
with Richard Weimer Gallery, Darien, Conn., sold in 1987 to NCF.

One of the most recent additions to the Newington-Cropsey Foundation's collection is *Lake Scene, Franconia Notch*, which is set in the White Mountains of New Hampshire in autumn. The promontory on the left may be Eagle Cliff, a well-known outcropping (shown in Cropsey's drawing *Eagle Cliffs, Franconia Notch*, 1852, NCF). This painting has none of the serenity and repose of Cropsey's *Lake George* (cat. no. 31), painted in the same year. The lonely, threatening landscape of *Lake Scene, Franconia Notch* recalls the work of Thomas Cole, for instance, *Landscape with Tree Trunks*, 1827–28 (Rhode Island School of Design, Providence). In both paintings, the dramatic elements of nature are emphasized—storm clouds, streaks of bright light, and high, jagged mountains.

   In *Lake Scene, Franconia Notch*, nature is both grand and ominous. The wind-torn trees serve as reminders of the violence that it can inflict, and the brooding clouds add another threatening note. The small scale of the deer underscores their vulnerability. Nevertheless, rays of light offer the hope that the storm will soon pass and nature will assume a gentler guise.

33. Paestum, *1871*

Oil on canvas, 17½ x 29½ in.
Signed and dated at lower right: J. F. Cropsey/1871

EX COLLECTION
with the Steinschneider family, to NCF.

In the 1870s, Jasper Cropsey painted a number of Italian scenes based on both his recollections of Italy and the drawings he had made there more than twenty years earlier. That he was still painting such views indicates the profound influence that Italy had on the artist. Works of the 1870s like *Temple of Ceres, Paestum*, 1875 (NCF), *The Campagna of Rome*, 1874 (Los Angeles County Museum), and *Paestum*, 1871, are dark and often dramatic. They are quite different from the picturesque, dreamy views that Cropsey painted in the 1850s, when his memories of Europe were fresh.

The temple depicted in *Paestum* cannot be identified specifically but certainly is based on one of the two Doric temples, of either Neptune or Ceres, and probably is a blending of the two. Like the earlier *Temple of Paestum, Crescent Moon* (cat. no. 28), the painting has a low vantage point and brilliant sunset sky. Cropsey has, however, intensified the dramatic effect of the later painting by focusing on a single temple, viewed closer and almost straight on, to increase the looming sense of its grandeur. The lonely, early evening mood of *Temple at Paestum, Crescent Moon* is replaced in *Paestum* by an apocalyptic sensation elicited by the vibrant blues, greens, and oranges of the sky and landscape and the bright light that falls over the front of the building. The composition is austere, consisting of broad bands of earth and sky, broken by the mass of the temple. Genre elements, the shepherd and the goats scampering among the ruins, serve as gentle reminders of present-day life and animate the desolate setting.

According to the illustrated catalog of the annual exhibition of the National Academy of Design, 1877, this painting was shown that year as *The Temple of Paestum* (no. 158, ill.) for sale by the artist.

34. River View II, *1871*

Oil on canvas, 12 x 20 in.
Signed and dated at lower right: J. F. Cropsey/1871

REFERENCES
John K. Howat, *The Hudson River and its Painters*, New York: American Legacy Press, 1972,
no. 70, ill., pp. 171–72, as *View of Catskills across Hudson*.
Nassau County Museum of Art, Roslyn, N.Y., *William Cullen Bryant and the Hudson River School
of Landscape Painting*, 1981, exhib. cat. by Holly J. Pinto, fig. 43, p. 15, as *View of Catskills across Hudson*.

EX COLLECTION
with Walter Wallace, New York, sold in 1953 to Mr. and Mrs. John C. Newington.

Although *River View I* (cat. no. 38) and *River View II* were painted three years apart, similarities in composition, size, coloring, and treatment make them convincing as a pair. The scenes have been identified as the Hudson River with the Catskill Mountains in the distance.[1] There is a strong emphasis on light not only in the sun's rays coming through the clouds but also in the sunset glow that pervades both pictures. The two paintings show Cropsey experimenting in more high-keyed colors, particularly in the sky. The sunset is rendered dramatically in yellows, blue-greens, and reds—all of which are picked up in the landscape, creating a unity of color.

1. Howat (1972), pp. 171–72, 178–79.

35. Church, Stoke Poges, *1872*

Oil on canvas, 22½ x 39½ in.
Signed and dated at lower left: J. F. Cropsey/1872

EX COLLECTIONS
sale of the estate of Frederic Frazier, Plaza Art Gallery, New York, April 30, 1943, no. 60, ill., as *Stoke Poges*.
with Leroy Ireland, Philadelphia, Pa.
with Savoy Art and Auction Galleries, New York, sold in 1951 to Mr. and Mrs. John C. Newington.

Saint Giles's church at Stoke Poges in England was the setting for Thomas Gray's famous poem "Elegy Written in a Country Churchyard," published in 1751. Jasper Cropsey painted the church at least five times prior to this version of 1872. The Plaza Art Gallery sale catalog identifies the scene as a wedding in the family of William Penn. In describing one of his paintings of the church, Cropsey stated that the poet Gray is "buried in the tomb under the church window upon which the figure is leaning. The tomb next [to] it is [Gray's] mother's. The Yew tree to the left is supposed to be the tree described as 'that Yew-Trees Shade, Where heaves the turf in many a mould'ring heap.'" Cropsey identified the land on the other side of the church wall as part of an estate that formerly belonged to William Penn.[1]

In *Church, Stoke Poges*, 1872, however, the figures in the wedding party and the influence of Gray's "Elegy" are secondary. The small figures are dominated by the landscape and the large building. Moreover, there is a strong pull, caused by the receding lines of the church wall and the pathway, that draws the viewer's gaze toward the church. Although the scene of the "Elegy," with its literary and historical significance, was attractive to Cropsey, his primary interest was in the church building as architecture. He focused his attention on the edifice and the precise rendering of its stonework and windows and the vines that cling to its walls. A steeple that had been added to Saint Giles's church in 1831 appears prominently in this painting. Interestingly, Cropsey's later painting *Summer (Stoke Poges)*, 1883 (cat. no. 44), shows the church without the steeple.

Church, Stoke Poges, 1872, is almost identical to an earlier view, *The Church at Stoke Poges*, 1864 (coll. Mrs. Deen Day Smith, Atlanta, Ga.), painted by Cropsey shortly after he returned to the United States from his second trip to England.

1. Description of a painting of the church at Stoke Poges, undated, Cropsey Papers, NCF, microfilm, roll 336, Arch. Am. Art.

36. Wooded Landscape, *1873*

Oil on canvas, 10 x 12 in.
Signed and dated at lower right: J. F. C./1873

EX COLLECTIONS
estate of the artist.
descended through family to NCF.

Wooded Landscape is a plein-air oil study of a rocky stream in the midst of a forest, one of many studies from nature made by Jasper Cropsey. They include *Tree Study*, 1848 (cat. no. 7), *Rock Study*, 1850 (cat. no. 10), and *Tree Study*, 1855 (cat. no. 22). In *Wooded Landscape*, thick paint and earthy colors are skillfully used to describe the textures of rock surfaces and tree trunks. Cropsey also captures the light that filters through the foliage and plays over the rocks and water. The viewer is confronted by objects close at hand, as in Cropsey's other studies. A screen of trees obstructs any view of deeper space. The result is an intimate glimpse of a densely wooded, not easily accessible spot, untouched by the manipulative hand of civilization.

Wooded Landscape resembles the plein-air studies of Asher B. Durand. For example, in *Study from Nature: Rocks and Trees*, 1856 (NYHS), Durand presents the landscape directly, allowing nature to provide the composition. Both Cropsey and Durand maintain a realist's approach to the subjects of their informal nature studies by not enhancing or beautifying the scene. Their studies record a glimpse of the fresh and vital natural world, as spontaneously revealed to each artist.

Concerning the inherent artistic elements in nature and the relationship between nature and God, Cropsey wrote, "I feel as if our hands should fall palsied at our sides and our intellects go wild when we cease to consider nature the 'monarch of all' in the truly worthy and beautiful in the fine arts. Why? Because she is the one great picture . . . painted for his praise and glory of which he said when he inscribed his matchless master name God upon it, 'He saw that it was good.'"[1]

1. J. Cropsey to J. M. Falconer, May 26, 1847, coll. Brown Reinhardt, Newark, Del., typescript, NCF.

37. Cold Spring on Hudson, *1874*

Oil on canvas, 11½ x 19½ in.
Signed and dated at lower right: J. F. Cropsey/1874

EX COLLECTION
with Richard Weimer Gallery, Darien, Conn., sold in 1985 to NCF.

The scene is a blustery day on the Hudson River near the town of Cold Spring, New York. In the second half of the nineteenth century, Cold Spring was a thriving manufacturing town, where the ironworks known as the West Point Foundry was located. This view seems to be looking downriver with the foundry dock and the buildings of Cold Spring partially visible on the left. On the right, the river bends around West Point, about a mile away.

Low, misty clouds over the Hudson Highlands are pierced by a crystalline light that floods the background and highlights the choppy water in the foreground. The effect is of a chilly, bright, and windy day in late autumn or early winter. One of the most distinctive features of *Cold Spring on Hudson* is the high degree of realism in the depiction of the water. By a subtle manipulation of tones, Cropsey shows the shadows of the clouds on the water and the translucence of the water in bright light.

38. River View I, *1874*

Oil on canvas, 12 x 20 in.
Signed and dated at lower left: J. F. Cropsey/1874

REFERENCES

John K. Howat, *The Hudson River and its Painters*, New York: American Legacy Press, 1972,
no. 81, ill., pp. 178–79, as *Sunset, Hudson River*.
Nassau County Museum of Art, Roslyn, N.Y., *William Cullen Bryant and the Hudson River School
of Landscape Painting*, 1981, exhib. cat. by Holly J. Pinto, fig. 42, p. 15, as *Sunset, Hudson River*.

EX COLLECTION

with Walter Wallace, New York, sold in 1953 to Mr. and Mrs. John C. Newington.

In their brilliant colors and thin paint, both *River View I* and *River View II* (cat. no. 34) resemble Cropsey's works in watercolor, such as *Lake Waywayanda*, 1881 (NCF). The watercolors, which are often Hudson River views, are characterized by nuances of color and light and by broad, open compositions.

39. Echo Lake—New Hampshire, *1875*

Oil on canvas, 14 x 23 in.
Signed and dated at lower right: J. F. Cropsey/1875

EX COLLECTIONS
with Adams Davidson Galleries, Washington, 1979.
with Robert Paul Weimann III, New Haven, Conn., sold in 1982 to NCF.

Reproduced in both the New York and London editions of the *Art Journal* of 1876, Jasper Cropsey's painting *Echo Lake—New Hampshire* has resurfaced only in the last decade. The scene is near Franconia Notch in the White Mountains. The rocky promontory on the left was identified by the London *Art Journal* as Eagle Cliff, an outcropping seen also in *Lake Scene, Franconia Notch* (cat. no. 32). The reviewer suggested that Echo Lake derived its name "from a remarkable echo which answers the slightest sound, and is repeated from crag to crag until lost in the distance."[1] The writer for the New York *Art Journal* was struck by the mood of the painting: "The artist has chosen the sunset hour for his picture, and has clothed it with much of the poetry and repose of the scene as they exist in Nature. The sun is just sinking behind the distant mountains, and its strong rays are suffused over every visible object, and blend all in one general glow of golden-toned light."[2]

Indeed, this warm, glowing light as well as the autumnal reds and oranges—all reflected in the still mountain pool—infuse the painting with an atmospheric glow. Despite the late afternoon haze, objects retain their detailed shapes and crisp outlines. For instance, the extraordinary cliffs are rendered with precision. Because the lake is enclosed by these rock precipices, with no open vista, a sense of solitude and seclusion pervades the picture. In such stillness, one might almost expect to hear the sound of the echo for which the lake was famous.

1. "Echo Lake," *Art Journal* (London), n.s. 15 (Nov. 1876), p. 332.
2. "Echo Lake," *Art Journal* (New York), n.s. 2 (Nov. 1876), p. 329.

40. Lake at Mount Chocorua, *1875*

Oil on canvas, 11⅝ x 19½ in.
Signed and dated at lower right: J. F. Cropsey/1875

Mount Chocorua, named for a chief of the Algonquian Indians, is the most spectacular peak of the Sandwich range in the White Mountains of New Hampshire. Sometimes compared to the Swiss Alps,[1] the area attracted artists of the Hudson River school, including John F. Kensett, Thomas Cole, Asher B. Durand, Albert Bierstadt, and Jasper F. Cropsey. There are many scenes of the White Mountains, especially Mount Chocorua, among Cropsey's works.

The view in *Lake at Mount Chocorua* is similar to that in two of his earlier works: a pencil drawing entitled *Mount Chocorua*, 1855 (NCF), and an oil painting entitled *Autumn—Chocorua Peak, White Mountains*, 1856 (private coll., New Hope, Pa.). In all three views, the mountain, with its unusual hooked peak, towers over a lake and dominates the landscape. In *Autumn—Chocorua Peak, White Mountains*, the dramatic characteristics of the landscape are emphasized; storm clouds stir overhead, and rocks and torn trees frame the view in the foreground. In the later *Lake at Mount Chocorua*, Cropsey does not focus on the on the awe-inspiring characteristics of the mountain; rather, he shows it at a distance, its unique form shrouded in a veil of haze.

1. John Disturnell, comp., *Travelers Guide to the Hudson River, Saratoga Springs, Lake George, Falls of Niagara and Thousand Islands* (New York: American News Company, 1864), p. 283.

41. Forty Steps, Newport, *1876*

Oil on canvas, 8¼ x 15¼ in.
Signed and dated at lower right: J. F. Cropsey/1876

EX COLLECTION
with Bodley Book Shop, New York, sold in 1947 to Mr. and Mrs. John C. Newington.

Forty Steps, Newport is an exquisitely colored and freely painted study of sky, water, and rocks. As in many of his paintings of the late 1870s and 1880s, Cropsey employs a horizontal format to study the effects of light on vast expanses of sky and water. The brilliant colors of the sunset still linger, while the moon throws shimmering light over the horizon, down the center of the picture, and onto the breaking waves.

Sunset on the Sea, 1872 (Metropolitan Museum of Art, New York), by John F. Kensett is similar to *Forty Steps, Newport*. Both artists use simple forms, vibrant colors reflected in the water and in the clouds, subtle lighting, and brushstrokes that convey the textures of the natural elements. The paintings seem to have been rapidly executed on the spot.

After seeing an earlier painting of the Forty Steps in Cropsey's studio, Henry T. Tuckerman said of the site, "More than one poet has sat there in reverie; more than one flirt has been awed into momentary earnestness by the limitless expanse of wave and sky thence stretching before her fickle eye; and many a rosy-cheeked urchin has gathered bright pebbles there and wet his little feet, while the nurse listened, forgetful of her charge, to an insinuating coachman."[1]

1. *Book of the Artists* (New York: G. P. Putnam and Sons, 1870), p. 539.

42. Storm with Sunburst over Catskills, *1876*

Oil on canvas, 8 x 14¾ in.
Signed and dated at lower left: J. F. Cropsey/1876

EX COLLECTIONS
with Taggert, Jorgensen, and Putnam Gallery, Washington.
with Richard Weimer Gallery, Darien, Conn., sold in 1984 to NCF.

One of Jasper F. Cropsey's most dramatic sunset paintings, *Storm with Sunburst over Catskills* is a study of the sky as sunlight pierces heavy clouds right after a storm. The intense reds and golds indicate that day is ending. Early in his career, Cropsey had become interested in the depiction of the sky at varying times of day and different seasons. In 1855, he wrote a sensitive essay called "Up among the Clouds" that described his observations of various effects of weather. He called the stormy sky, with sun beams flickering through it, "a sky more pictorial than all others."[1] Titles like *Twilight, after a Rainy Day, Study of Sun-Set—Storm Sky,* and *Study of Sky—Sun-Rise* in the sale catalogs of Cropsey's later works indicate that he continued to produce numerous sky studies.[2]

Because of its small size and free and rapid execution, *Storm with Sunburst over Catskills* must itself be a study. It bears a strong resemblance to an oil sketch dated 1860, *Sunset after a Storm in the Catskills* (Detroit Institute of Arts). The dramatic sunset sky in the 1860 work has been compared to the sky in Frederic E. Church's *Twilight in the Wilderness,* 1860 (Cleveland Museum of Art).[3] Clearly, in both studies, Cropsey captured the sublime drama and vibrant color of Church's landscape vision together with his own careful study of the sky.

1. "Up among the Clouds," *Crayon* 2 (August 8, 1855), pp. 79–80.
2. Messrs. Foster, London, *A Catalogue of a Collection of Finished Pictures and Sketches of that Talented American Artist, J. F. Cropsey, Esq.,* April 29, 1863, and John T. Boyd, auctioneer, Warwick, N.Y., *Chattel Mortgage Sale of the Effects of Jasper F. Cropsey, Esq., Artist,* Oct. 30–31, 1884.
3. Graham Hood, "American Paintings Acquired During the Last Decade," *Bulletin of the Detroit Institute of Arts* 55, no. 2 (1977), p. 87.

43. Cows in Landscape, *1880*

Oil on canvas, 12 x 20 in.
Signed and dated at lower right: J. F. Cropsey/1880

EX COLLECTIONS
with Sotheby's, New York.
with Ira Spanierman Gallery, New York.
with Richard Weimer Gallery, Darien, Conn., sold in 1983 to NCF.

Jasper F. Cropsey's American landscapes usually feature cows—grazing or wading in water, singly or in small groups—whereas his European views show goats and sheep. In *Cows in Landscape* there are three cows beside a river, perhaps the Hudson. It is dotted with sailboats, another recurring motif, which Cropsey had taken up in the 1860s. This quiet, pastoral scene has none of the theatrical lighting or vibrant colors that he frequently used in his later works. Instead, *Cows in Landscape* is reminiscent of his much earlier landscapes, for instance, *Chenango River, New York*, 1856 (cat. no. 23), and *Springtime on the Hudson*, 1856 (cat. no. 24). In all three landscapes, the colors are subdued and earthy, and the lighting is bright, as at midday.

44. Four Seasons, *1883*

Spring (Mediterranean)
Summer (Stoke Poges)
Autumn (Lake George)
Winter (Simplon Pass)

Oil on canvas, 4 x 8¼ in. each, framed together
Signed and dated individually: J. F. Cropsey/1883

EX COLLECTION
with Richard Weimer Gallery, Darien, Conn., sold in 1985 to NCF.

Jasper Cropsey's account books do not mention any series of paintings of the seasons until the mid-1850s, when sales of three sets are recorded.[1] A set of the four seasons dated between 1859 and 1861 (coll. Stuart P. Feld, New York) is closely related in format and iconography to *Four Seasons*, 1883. In both, Cropsey used locations in Europe and America. Not surprisingly, because of the renown of America's fall foliage and his reputation for skillfully representing it, Cropsey chose American scenery for *Autumn*. In the series *Four Seasons*, 1883, the autumn scene is of Lake George in Warren County, New York. It shows the lake surrounded by dense forest and mountains, with storm clouds overhead, and is quite different from the open expanse of still water and clear, bright sky in Cropsey's 1870 *Lake George* (cat. no. 31). The three other locations in *Four Seasons*, 1883, had been visited by Cropsey during his first trip to Europe, from 1847 to 1849. They are the coast of Italy (*Spring*), Stoke Poges in England (*Summer*), and the Simplon Pass in Switzerland (*Winter*). There are figures in these three scenes. In *Spring*, presumably a view of the Bay of Naples, a pair of lovers, juxtaposed to a statue of two lovers, look out to sea. In *Winter*, figures on foot and on horseback trek through the Simplon Pass. In *Summer*, figures walk through the churchyard of Saint Giles's church in Stoke Poges. The view is identical to that of *Church, Stoke Poges*, 1883 (NCF). In both, Cropsey omits the church steeple that had been erected in 1831 and that appears in *Church, Stoke Poges*, 1872 (cat. no. 35).

The small paintings in *Four Seasons*, shown here, may be studies for another set, one of which possibly is *Church, Stoke Poges*, 1883 (NCF).

1. Cropsey's account book, 1845–1868, Cropsey Papers, NCF, microfilm, roll 336, Arch. Am. Art.

Four Seasons — Spring (Mediterranean)

Four Seasons — Summer (Stoke Poges)

Four Seasons — Autumn (Lake George)

Four Seasons — Winter (Simplon Pass)

45. Cows on River, *1887*

Oil on canvas, 11¾ x 19¾ in.
Signed and dated at lower left: J. F. Cropsey/1887

Cows on River is a softly brushed and thinly painted view of an unidentified river with low mountains and a broad sky, dotted with puffy cumulous clouds. Three cows wade in the shallow waters on the left, and a man rows a boat in the middle distance. This quiet midday or afternoon scene is reminiscent of river views by Asher B. Durand, such as *Summer Afternoon*, 1865 (Metropolitan Museum of Art, New York). Like Durand's, Cropsey's painting is peaceful and still. Warm light, reflected by the motionless water, infuses the scene. Rather than the subdued earth tones employed by Durand, however, Cropsey uses brilliant reds and yellows in the sky and the landscape. *Cows on River*, both in its colors and simple, open composition, is similar to Cropsey's earlier painting with cows entitled *Upper Hudson*, 1871 (NCF).

46. Winter on the Hudson, *1887*

Oil on canvas, 11½ x 19¾ in.
Signed and dated at lower right: J. F. Cropsey/1887

EX COLLECTIONS
Cropsey sale, Ortgies and Company, New York, March 31, 1887, no. 54, as *Ice in the Hudson
River*, 12 x 20 in. (probably this painting).
with Richard Weimer Gallery, Darien, Conn., sold in 1984 to NCF.

In 1884, because of financial difficulties, Jasper Cropsey was forced to sell his home Aladdin, near Warwick, New York. The following year, he bought a smaller house in Hastings-on-Hudson and added a studio similar to the one he had built at Aladdin. The new home, which the Cropseys called Ever Rest, had a splendid view of the Hudson River and the Palisades. Therefore, it is hardly surprising that the river became the primary subject of Cropsey's paintings from 1885 until his death. *Winter on the Hudson* shows the river at sunset. The entire foreground is water and large chunks of ice, on which small white birds rest. The bright light of the setting sun and the vibrant colors of the sky are reflected by the river, creating a unity of tone across the canvas. In the dramatic, cloud-streaked sky (which resembles Frederic E. Church's treatment), rows of dark clouds alternate with bright reds, pinks, purples, silvers, and golds—setting the entire work aglow.

Winter on the Hudson, or a similar painting by Cropsey, received strong praise in 1894:

> It is a picture of the lordly river filled with drift ice, which has become linked together by a newly frozen 'crop.' The hills in the distance are covered with snow, and the foreground is animated by the presence of snow birds. A strong light is poured by the sun on the landscape, causing the ice to become opalescent and to shine with tints characteristic of Bradford's famous arctic scenes and even, it might seem, like the waters of Venice under the gaze of Turner! . . . it is Cropsey at such a degree of perfection that one marvels how the master of autumn scenes can become an expert at depicting winter, too.[1]

1. J. Perry Worden, "Some Thoughts on Art. Number Ten. Cropsey, the Artist of Nature," May 5, 1894, possibly the *Gazette*, a clipping in Cropsey Papers, NCF, microfilm, Arch. Am. Art.

47. Hudson River at Hastings, *1889*

Oil on canvas, 8⅛ x 19⅝ in.
Signed and dated at lower left: J. F. Cropsey/1889

REFERENCE
Cleveland Museum of Art, Munson-Williams-Proctor Institute, Utica, N.Y., and National Collection
of Fine Arts, Smithsonian Institution, Washington, traveling exhib., 1970–71,
Jasper F. Cropsey, 1823–1900, cat. by William S. Talbot, no. 75, p. 106.

Hastings-on-Hudson, where Jasper F. Cropsey lived from 1885 until his death in 1900, is on the east side of the Hudson River. The view in *Hudson River at Hastings* is from a point downriver so that the town appears at the right. The scene is busy, with boats traveling the river as far as the eye can see and smoke billowing from the Hastings factories. The inclusion of industrial elements is unusual in Cropsey's river views and other landscapes; but, like the train in *Study for "Starrucca Viaduct—Autumn"* (cat. no. 26), the factories here are unobtrusive. They are situated close to the horizon where they blend into the surroundings, and the smoke from their tall smokestacks dissipates readily in the cloudy sky. The stacks themselves echo the masts of the nearby sailboats.

Hudson River at Hastings was modeled on a watercolor of the same title, 1886 (NCF), made by Cropsey the year after he moved to Hastings.[1]

1. William S. Talbot, *Jasper F. Cropsey, 1823–1900* (Ph.D. diss., Institute of Fine Arts, New York University, 1972; published New York: Garland Publishing, 1977), p. 473.

48. Sunset on the Palisades, Hastings, *1890*

Oil on canvas, 13½ x 23⅜ in.
Signed and dated at lower right: J. F. Cropsey/1890

REFERENCE
Nassau County Museum of Art, Roslyn, N.Y., *William Cullen Bryant and the Hudson River School of Landscape Painting*, 1981, exhib. cat. by Holly J. Pinto, no. 11, ill.

A grand display of color and light, *Sunset on the Palisades, Hastings* is a stunning example of Cropsey's sunset views, a summation of the many glorious late afternoons that he witnessed from his house above the Hudson River. His interest in the depiction of the sky, clouds, and especially sunsets is here given full orchestration. The rendering is similar to that of Frederic E. Church in *Sunset*, 1856 (Munson-Williams-Proctor Institute, Utica, N.Y.). In both paintings, the clouds are in riblike configurations, parallel to the horizon. They are underlighted by the last rays of the sun, and their colors deepen with their distance from the sun. These sunset skies are so dramatic that details of the landscape become secondary to the abstract elements of color and design.

49. Twilight

Oil on cardboard, 6½ x 11 in.
Not signed or dated

This late study shows Jasper Cropsey experimenting with the abstract properties of color, light, and form. *Twilight* consists almost entirely of sky, with a mountain landscape in the lower third of the picture. Earth and sky are suggested by the abstract application of color, and shapes are delineated mainly by brushwork. The dark foreground brightens into a horizon lighted by the last rays of the sun. Night encroaches at the upper edge of the picture.

Beginning in the 1860s, Cropsey painted a large number of seasonal and temporal studies. Their simplification and lack of detail carried over into the finished paintings of his later years, for example, *Forty Steps, Newport*, 1876 (cat. no. 41). Dispensing with boats, figures, and trees, Cropsey was free to investigate the expressive qualities of color and light. The freedom in the application of the paint, the brilliant coloring, and the abstract appearance of the landscape suggest that *Twilight* is a work of the 1890s.

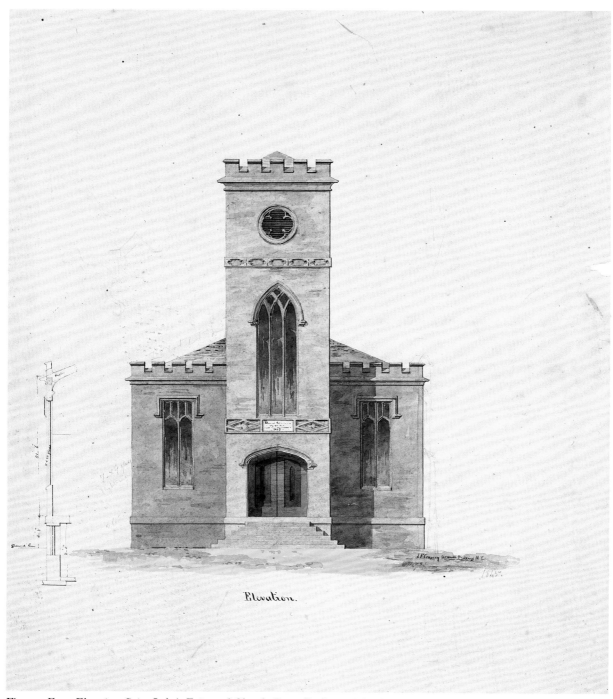

Elevation.

Fig. 1: *Front Elevation, Saint Luke's Episcopal Church, Rossville, Staten Island,* 1845, watercolor and pencil on paper, 13 x 10¾ in., signed and dated at lower right: J. F. Cropsey. Granite Building, N.Y./1845. Newington-Cropsey Foundation.

Jasper F. Cropsey: Architect

BY BARBARA FINNEY

To most of his contemporaries, Jasper F. Cropsey's name evoked landscape painting, not architecture. Today, more than one hundred recently cataloged architectural drawings have revealed a new facet of Cropsey's artistic talent. Included are elevations, presentation drawings, floor plans, sections, and working drawings for rural and urban projects.[1] The present exhibition displays a small portion of this rich heritage of nineteenth-century architectural images.

Most of the designs were executed between 1863 and 1887 and mirror the eclecticism of that period. In his rural and cottage plans Cropsey (1823–1900) seems to have been particularly guided by the picturesque bracketed modes of the architectural theorist and landscape gardener Andrew Jackson Downing (1815–52) and the architect Calvert Vaux (1824–95). Like the Victorian tastemaker John Ruskin (1819–1900), Cropsey believed that surface ornamentation and texture were of paramount importance. Nonetheless, Ruskin would have deplored the outcome of Cropsey's major architectural commission: fourteen elevated railway stations, built of standardized iron components in New York in 1878. "True architecture," Ruskin declared in *Seven Lamps of Architecture*, "does not admit of iron as a constructive material," nor, to him, was machine ornamentation ever an acceptable substitute for the work of the hand.[2]

Because they were usually not valued, countless nineteenth-century architectural drawings have been lost or destroyed. The Newington-Cropsey Foundation's collection is rare, not only because of the number of drawings involved but also because they can be confidently ascribed to one architect. Through these works, Cropsey's growing skills as a draftsman and watercolorist can be charted during the same period in which he was also developing as a landscape artist.

A five-year apprenticeship from 1837 to 1842 with the New York architect Joseph Trench (1815–79) laid the foundation for Cropsey's unusual dual career. His aptitude for drawing landscapes and botanical subjects was sharpened by the precision and concentration required in architectural draftsmanship. He learned to use watercolor to depict minute detail and in broad washes of color. As his drawing and painting skills developed, they inevitably played a role in improving his architectural work. His perspective drawings after 1866, for example, exemplify the artistic expression and freedom that was, according to *American Architect and Building News*, more essential to the architect than mechanical accuracy in drawing.[3]

Cropsey's architectural drawings fall into the two categories—objective and subjective—set forth by the English architect Reginald Blomfield (1856–1942) in *Architectural Drawing and Draftsmen*.[4] Objective, two-dimensional works included working drawings, elevations, floor plans, and sections useful primarily to the builder. Subjective works encompassed the architect's roughly sketched original ideas and the presentation views that were meant to give the client a three-dimensional impression of the completed project. Here, a variety of techniques, dramatic settings, and artistic and atmospheric effects were permitted.

In a large firm such as that of H. H. Richardson (1838–86) the design process was shared. It began with an idea conceived by the master, which was translated by assistants into a sequence of drawings. Cropsey, on the other hand, worked alone. He formulated all his designs by himself—except those for the passenger stations of the Gilbert Elevated Railway. Due to the technological complexity of that project, individual drawings were prepared under Cropsey's supervision by draftsmen and engineers employed by the iron fabricator, the J. B. and J. W. Cornell Company in New York. Usually, Cropsey competed single-handedly against architects who employed the specialized help necessitated by the diversity of post-Civil War building types and rising professional standards.[5] His output should therefore be judged in this context.

Of his urban projects, only two are known to have been carried out: the Gilbert passenger stations and a decorative scheme for the Seventh Regiment Armory in 1879. Cropsey also designed five town houses between 1866 and 1873 and an early apartment building in 1867. Probably intended for New York, they were apparently never built.[6] Such designs, however, indicate that Cropsey had strong urban ties in addition to his well-documented identification with rural and wilderness America.[7]

Jasper Cropsey's architectural apprenticeship was more rigorous than that of artists such as Thomas Cole (1801–48), John Trumbull (1756–1843), and Samuel F. B. Morse (1791–1872), who also pursued architecture. In Trench's office, Cropsey first studied geometry and draftsmanship. He later wrote that, after eighteen months, "scarcely a finished drawing left the office without passing through my hands." By his fourth year he had progressed to painting watercolor backgrounds in architectural designs. The works he saw at the annual National Academy of Design exhibitions in New York stimulated his independent studies of linear perspective and "the theory of light and shadow."[8] Both were useful—in art and in preparing presentation views for architectural projects. Cropsey's landscape painting was greatly encouraged by his employer. This enthusiasm may have reflected Trench's interest in the work of a famous competitor, the New York architect and draftsman Alexander Jackson Davis (1803–92). Davis's name was well known, in part for the delicate, three-dimensional, hand-colored lithographs that illustrated his 1837 book *Rural Residences* and also for his later plans done in collaboration with Andrew Jackson Downing. *Rural Residences* presented designs for villas and cottages, which in their asymmetry, varied outlines, and textures brilliantly conveyed the qualities of picturesque architecture. In all but one design, buildings were linked to their surroundings by means of sky, trees, and shrubbery.[9]

Cropsey's training appears to have been of high caliber even though Trench, only twenty-two years old in 1837, was apparently just launching his career.[10] However, in late 1841 or early 1842 Cropsey left Trench's employ and set up his own office at 72 Chambers Street. A record of his accounts suggests that for a time he may have continued to accept low-paying drafting jobs from his former employer.[11] Cropsey's first independent commission was a Greek Revival church at New Dorp, Staten Island. His side elevation in sparce watercolor (plate 1) shows a simple, severe structure in keeping with the austerity of the Moravian sect. The "Principal Plan," placing the pews and pulpit, and the "Gallery Plan" that Cropsey prepared for the church are his first known plans showing the arrangement of interior space. Saint Luke's Episcopal Church (fig. 1), built at Rossville, Staten Island, in 1845, is the only other early commission for which plans survive. Using a more fluid watercolor technique, Cropsey depicted an Early Gothic Revival facade with a projecting, crenelated tower and a tall lancet window divided by tracery. The quatrefoil motif that appears in a circular window in the top register became one of Cropsey's trademarks. The interior of the church was quite elegant, containing groin-vaulted aisles and slender compound piers.

Cropsey and his wife, Maria, were in Europe from 1847 to 1849 and again from 1856 to 1863. During the first trip, Cropsey's focus was the picturesque classical and medieval sites of Italy, England, and Scotland that inspired many mid-century American artists and art patrons. He also, however, observed and sketched monuments purely as architecture. The annotations "Architectural Antiquities of Great Britain" and "Ancient Ecclesiastical Architecture" scattered among Cropsey's notebook studies of Italy refer to influential books by John Britton. In an 1848 pocket notebook Cropsey made thumbnail sketches of classical temple forms and correctly labeled them *dipteral*, *pseudodipteral*, *amphidistyle*, and *peripteral*.[12]

In England and Scotland, it was the Gothic Revival that made the deepest impression on him. Like thousands of other tourists stirred by romantic associations, Cropsey visited Abbotsford, Sir Walter Scott's castellated mansion near Melrose Abbey. His sketch, made in July 1847, of the ruins of Jedburgh Abbey, Roxburghshire, Scotland (Metropolitan Museum of Art, New York), was one of many drawings that portray architectural sites as both romantic ruins and architectonic structures. Cropsey arrived in London not long after construction began on the new Houses of Parliament, which replaced those razed by fire in 1834. The buildings, designed by Sir Charles Barry (1795–1860) and A. W. N. Pugin (1812–52), were, Cropsey wrote, "one of the most beautiful pieces of workmanship in existence."[13] The rich late Gothic

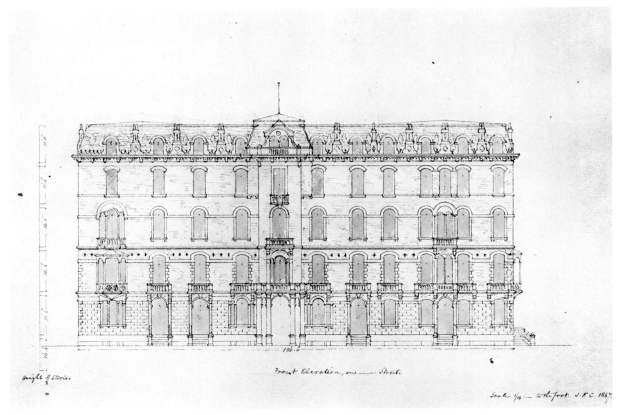

Fig. 2: *Front Elevation, Apartment Building*, 1867, watercolor and colored inks on paper, 8¼ x 11¾ in., signed and dated at lower right: J. F. C. 1867. Newington-Cropsey Foundation.

detailing, designed by Pugin, reflected the growing taste for the picturesque in architecture and ornamentation. A suggestion of other sources of influence on Cropsey as an architect are found in the detailed sketches of capitals at Durham Castle that he preserved in a notebook. They are annotated with references to specific pages in Ruskin's *Stones of Venice* and to Thomas Rickman, whose volume *An Attempt to Discriminate the Styles of Architecture in England* was autographed by Cropsey and is now in his library at Hastings-on-Hudson.[14]

In 1863, Jasper Cropsey returned to the United States from his last trip abroad. His reputation as a painter of American scenes appeared secure, but he was deeply in debt. We learn from his papers that, beginning in 1863, he sometimes repaid loans from art patrons by rendering architectural services.[15] In 1866, he executed one of his first formal designs since 1845: a watercolor elevation of a brick-fronted town house with an awkwardly proportioned mansard (NCF). Its restrained Gothic detailing includes stone hood moldings, asymmetrically placed windows, a three-story bay, and a decorative band of crosses cut into the facade. The drawing is rather stiff; but, despite the density of thickly shadowed areas and the use of a straight-edge for outlining, it gives evidence—in the rich textures of slate, glass, stone, and brick—of Cropsey's growth as a watercolorist. An unfinished design, also dated 1866, shows a palette and brush as the whimsical finial on a second-story oriel (plate 2). This suggests that the plan was intended for two lots Cropsey bought that year on West Forty-ninth Street.[16]

Throughout the 1860s, urban congestion, inadequate housing, and unsanitary conditions were urgent problems. Yet middle-class Victorian morality was offended by the concept of the apartment house in which separate families would live under the same roof. Nonetheless, in 1867 Cropsey was commissioned by an art patron, George B. Warren, to design a twenty-unit apartment building. It was hoped that with shrubbery and fountains the outcome would resemble an elegant European public building. Had it been built, the five-story Second Empire structure would have predated by two years the acclaimed "first" apartment house, the Stuyvesant, designed by Richard Morris Hunt (1827–95) in 1869.

Cropsey's preliminary street elevation (fig. 2), which was apparently never carried further, displayed asymmetrically placed doors and windows, which were unusual for the Second Empire mode. The plans included an inner court reached by a carriage drive (plate 3). The same idea occurred to Hunt in designing the Stuyvesant but was rejected. With a rusticated ground level and first-floor quoins, balconies, and complex window groupings, the building lightened as it ascended toward a decorative mansard. The first two stories were imaginatively divided into seven duplex apartments linked by private stairways. Kitchens, bathrooms, dining rooms, storerooms, servants' quarters, and sculleries were on the ground floor; parlors, studies, and bedrooms were above, on the first floor.

In the 1870s, Cropsey's town-house elevations became increasingly flamboyant and were enlivened with ornamental surface detailing such as his own intertwined initials, incised floral forms, and decorative ironwork.[17] In 1871 and 1873, he drew two similar elevations that combined Gothic and Queen Anne Revival elements with unusual freedom (plate 4 and fig. 3). They are dominated by large studios and may have been inspired by the novel, urban studio-homes designed in London in the early 1870s by Philip Webb (1831–1915).

In 1866 Cropsey had purchased forty acres of land in rural Orange County, two miles from Warwick, New York. It was situated not far from the Greenwood Lake area where he had met his wife. Construction of a twenty-nine-room summer residence named Aladdin (fig. 4) was begun in 1867. In size, lavishness, and setting, the completed home competed with Frederic E. Church's Olana at Hudson, New York, and Albert Bierstadt's Malkasten at Irvington-on-Hudson. A major feature of Aladdin was a studio wing thirty feet square, with a cupola to admit light into the painting room (fig. 5). Broad landscaped vistas, curved driveways, and a tall, medievalized, mansarded entrance tower had an imposing effect on visitors. A jagged

Fig. 3: *Front Elevation, City House*, 1873, watercolor and ink on paper, 22 x 17½ in., signed and dated at lower right: J. F. Cropsey 1873. M. & M. Karolik Collection. Courtesy of Museum of Fine Arts, Boston.

Fig. 4: *Front Elevation, Aladdin*, preliminary drawing, 1866, ink with colored washes heightened with white on paper, 12½ x 19¼ in., signed and dated lower right: J. F. C. 1866. Newington-Cropsey Foundation.

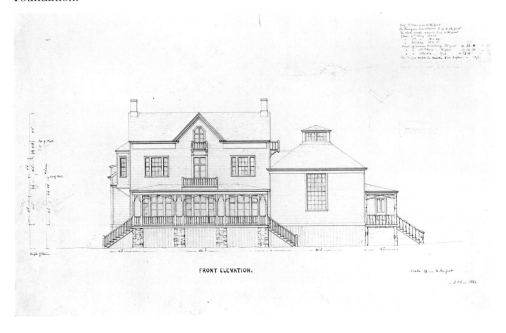

Fig. 5: *Interior of My Studio at Warwick, from 1869 to 1885*, watercolor and pencil on paper,
11 in. square. Newington-Cropsey Foundation.

roof line, numerous verandas, overhanging eaves and projections, vertical board-and-batten sheathing, and informally arranged interior space are clearly indebted to the bracketed modes popularized by Downing and Vaux. The outcome, in fact, seemed to exemplify Downing's belief that "the man of sentiment or feeling and the man of imagination are the men for picturesque villas, country houses with high roofs, steep gables, unsymmetrical and capricious forms. The architect may safely introduce tower and capanile—any and every feature that indicates boldness, energy and variety of character."[18]

In 1874 the railroad car magnate George M. Pullman (1831–97), whom Cropsey probably met after the Civil War, commissioned him to design a vacation home. It was to be a fourteen-room, ocean-front villa at Long Branch, New Jersey, near the "Summer White House" purchased for President Ulysses S. Grant in 1869 by a group of wealthy businessmen, including Pullman. Throughout 1874, Cropsey was immersed in Pullman's project. He designed plans, wrote specifications, let bids, and supervised construction at the Ocean Avenue site, traveling from New York at least once with General Horace Porter, Pullman's emissary and vice-president of the Pullman Palace Car Company of Detroit. Like Aladdin, the Pullman house included a commanding central tower with a mansard culminating in ornate cresting. To take advantage of the sea air, Cropsey also designed encircling "piazzas," or verandas—features in which Pullman was particularly interested.[19] The impressionistic, unfinished quality of Cropsey's perspective view of the Pullman villa (fig. 6) foreshadowed the looser, lighter rendering that he began to use in architectural drawing in the mid-1870s. Detail is suppressed in favor of the general impression of the completed house *in situ*. Economy of means extends even to the setting. For example, a sense of the seaside is conveyed merely by accentuated chalky highlights and contrasting shadows.

One of Cropsey's most beautiful architectural images (fig. 7) probably dates to this period. Posing the house against empty space and using washes of luminous watercolor with no

Fig. 6: *Elevation, Mrs. Pullman's Villa at Long Branch*, 1873, ink, pencil, colored washes, heightened with white on yellow-gray paper, 6½ x 6½ in., signed and dated at lower right: J. F. Cropsey 1873. M. & M. Karolik Collection. Courtesy of Museum of Fine Arts, Boston.

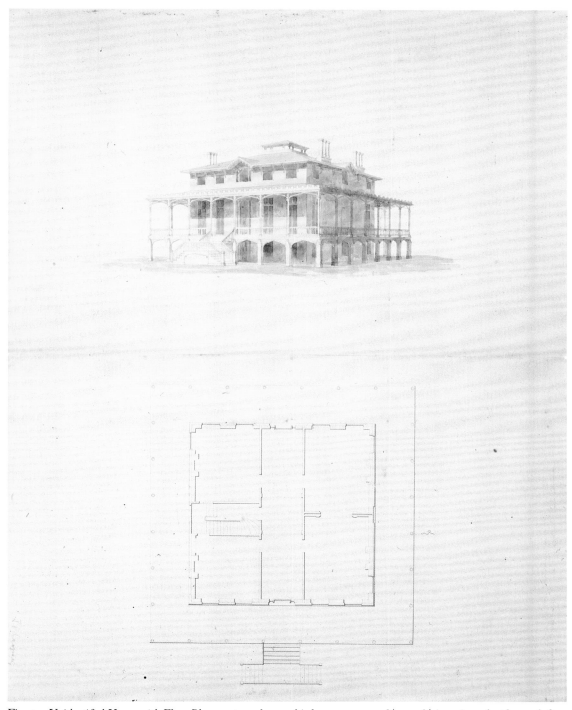

Fig. 7: *Unidentified House with Floor Plan*, watercolor and ink on paper, 2 1¾ x 1 7¾ in., signed at lower left: J. F. Cropsey. Newington-Cropsey Foundation.

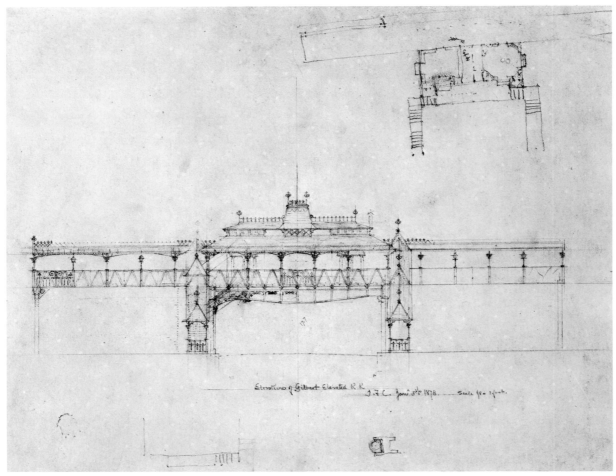

Fig. 8: *Design for Elevation of Gilbert Elevated Railroad*, pencil on paper, 19¼ x 26 in., signed and dated at lower center: J. F. C. Jan. 5th 1878. M. & M. Karolik Collection. Courtesy of Museum of Fine Arts, Boston.

hard-edge delineation, he blends architecture with art. On the other hand, an unfinished sketch of details, drawn in pencil and marked "Gen. Horace Porter's House" (NCF), is an example of Cropsey's love of such ornamentation as quatrefoils, Eastlake-type perforations, and the patterns created by juxtaposed horizontal and vertical siding. The effect was of surface fragmentation, which masked a block-like underlying structure reminiscent of the Greek Revival of Cropsey's apprenticeship period.

In 1867, despite the example of London's successful underground system, New York became the first city in the world to develop a mass-transit network based on elevated railways. That year an experimental half-mile track was tested on Greenwich Street. From 1871 to 1878, the New York Elevated Railroad Company offered passenger service along a limited route on Ninth Avenue. It was not until 1875, following the appointment of a powerful Board of Rapid Transit Commissioners, that the decision was made to go forward with a comprehensive metropolitan system. Initially, two lines were approved—the New York Elevated, with its growing Ninth Avenue route, and the Gilbert Elevated Railway Company, franchised to operate along Sixth and Second avenues. The latter's principal route, on Sixth Avenue, began at Rector Street near Trinity Episcopal Church and ended at Fifty-ninth Street, at the southern boundary of Central Park.[20]

Jasper Cropsey's winning sketch for the Gilbert elevated station pavilion (fig. 8), dated January 5, 1878, became the model for fourteen fire-resistant, galvanized-iron stations. It shows that Cropsey, working virtually without precedents, solved the problem of passenger access from street to track level in a picturesque but practical way. The scheme resulted in the first architecturally noteworthy passenger facilities built in America for modern urban mass transit. Until demolished by the La Guardia Administration in 1939, Cropsey's pavilions served millions of New Yorkers.

In retrospect, Cropsey's role as architect-designer, responsible for all "drawings, sketches and directions" and daily supervision of exterior and interior planning,[21] can be explained on the basis of his contacts with Pullman and Porter. Pullman, the major financial backer of the Gilbert line, and Porter, its vice-president, were in a position to influence the railroad's board of directors in Cropsey's favor, even though several prominent architects were still under consideration in late January 1878.[22]

Cropsey's accomplishment is clear when his design is compared to the earliest elevated stations, built between 1868 and 1878. At best, these were nineteenth-century train depots raised to track height. Cropsey's stations, on the other hand, provided airy track-level loggias that overlooked the streets below; while inside, the separate, gas-heated male and female waiting rooms with lavatories were conveniences unknown to horsecar passengers. When the line was inaugurated on June 5, 1878, the unfinished buildings were scenes of vigorous activity as people clambered aboard the trains for a free ride.[23]

Juxtaposed to the ugliness of unregulated urban sprawl, Cropsey's ornate, light-green, iron facades with gilded finials had immense appeal.[24] The square entrance kiosks (fig. 9) were decorated with tracery and scrollwork, large quatrefoils with circles punched from cast iron, pierced work, bold diamond shapes, and colonnettes with composite capitals. The free, serpentine pattern and flat, surface quality of the scrolls portended the earliest stages of art nouveau, and it is quite possible that Cropsey was aware of similar developments in the decorative work of such English designers as William Morris (1834–96) and Christopher Dresser (1834–1904). In the words of a writer for *Frank Leslie's Illustrated Newspaper*, the station exteriors with their

Fig. 9: Kiosk, Gilbert Elevated Railway, Sixth Avenue Line, 50th Street Station, 1913, albumen print, 9½ x 7⅝ in. Herman Cos, photographer. The New-York Historical Society.

"many gables, ventilators, [and] finials" resembled "a modification of the Renaissance and Gothic styles of architecture, presenting somewhat the appearance of a Swiss villa."[25]

While the facades displayed a highly irregular silhouette from certain angles, the basic station plan was predicated on a simple rectangle. A central passage containing the ticket booth led to a platform between waiting rooms on either side. Although the laciness of their design gave the buildings an appearance of floating above the street, this impression was counterbalanced by the iron superstructure and the anchor of the kiosks and stairways.

The contemporary Eastlake style, widely popularized in America through Charles Locke Eastlake's *Hints on Household Tastes in Furniture, Upholstery and Other Details* (Boston, 1872), inspired Cropsey's practical, crowd-pleasing waiting rooms. They were furnished with black-walnut seats and countertops, and the walls were decorated with walnut bands and quatrefoil motifs "touched with paint inside."[26] Floors had wood strips of alternating walnut and ash and were centered with large ash squares. Ceiling ventilators were inset with triangles of purple, green, and amber stained glass. Each waiting room was illuminated with gas chandeliers "worth twenty dollars a piece."[27] At night, the light from glass lamps and globes on side brackets imparted a festive air to the platforms.

Originally, the stations were resisted by Sixth Avenue merchants. Their attitudes changed when positive effects on commerce were noted. In June 1878, for example, the *New York Times* reported a surge of patrons to the restaurants around the Rector Street stop. The crunch of people on side streets adjacent to other stations was said to "gladden the shopkeeper's eye."[28]

In 1879, Cropsey volunteered to design and supervise the decoration of the ceiling and balconies of the drill room (plates 5 and 6) of the Seventh Regiment Armory at Park Avenue and Sixty-seventh Street in New York. The armory had been designed in 1876 by Charles W. Clinton, and the size of the drill room alone—298 feet by 187 feet—was staggering. The program of patriotic motifs and floral interlaces was set forth in specifications written in Cropsey's own hand and executed according to his full-scale paper patterns.[29] Panels between rafters were to be painted with "8 courses" of "emblematical" figures and "line work, in rich colors," as noted in the specifications. These included wide bands of stars, shields, stylized flowers, and sinuous scrollwork in varied hues. One pattern, which combines abstract designs and organic forms in such a way that new scrolls seem to sprout from every corner, suggests a further development toward early art nouveau. Apparently the project was not regarded as

Fig. 10: *Waldheim*, 1887, watercolor on paper, 10 x 16 in., signed and dated at lower center: Waldheim/Residence of W. H. Webb, Esq./J. F. C. 1887 Oct 4th. Newington-Cropsey Foundation.

particularly noteworthy because, in comparison to Louis C. Tiffany (1812–1902) and the Associated Artists who were paid $20,000 for decorating the veterans' room and library, Cropsey's donated services seem to have received little acknowledgment.

Cropsey's last commission as an architect was received from W. H. Webb[30] at Tarrytown, New York, for a residence to be called Waldheim. The design, possibly intended as a summer home, made wide use of Queen Anne Revival features. There were materials of varied textures, a multi-gabled roof, bays and other projections, a polygonal turret, and narrow clustered chimneys. A watercolor view, dated October 1887 (fig. 10), surrounds the building with a framework of the vivid fall foliage for which Cropsey was famous as a painter. It is one of his most improvisational architectural drawings and gauges the distance traveled from his first watercolor attempts in the mid-1840s.

After Jasper Cropsey's death on June 22, 1900, an obituary in the *New York Times* praised the Gilbert Elevated Railway stations. It cited their artistic and decorative merits and Cropsey's solution to a difficult problem.[31] All of his architectural experience—early training, European study, and the commissions that taught him facility in functional planning—coalesced in this achievement. His inventive approach to decoration appealed to the opulent tastes of the period and played a major role in his success.

When Cropsey began work in the field of architecture, a few building types were sufficient to meet the needs of a simpler society. The Greek and Gothic revivals were dominant. By the time he resumed his career in 1863, the High Victorian Gothic prevailed in institutional and ecclesiastical architecture, while eclecticism reigned in domestic building design. New materials and more complex building types were a challenge to every architect. Cropsey met the challenge with a unique station design that symbolized the new age of rapid transit. Much of his architecture was intended for personal use. Because of this, he was not subject to the constraints of a professional practice. Therefore, he was occasionally able to break through the thin boundaries of historical revivalism to create ornamentation that gives hints of art nouveau.

Cropsey's architectural drawings shed new light on the creative life of a Hudson River school landscape painter. Furthermore, they are important visual documents of eclecticism in nineteenth-century American architecture, as seen through the eyes of an artist.

NOTES

1. The bulk of Cropsey's architectural drawings have been preserved at Ever Rest, his last studio, at Hastings-on-Hudson, N.Y., now the Newington-Cropsey Foundation, hereafter referred to as NCF. Other drawings are in the M. & M. Karolik Collection, Museum of Fine Arts, Boston. The earliest systematic discussion of his architecture is in William S. Talbot's pioneering study *Jasper F. Cropsey, 1823–1900* (Ph.D. diss., Institute of Fine Arts, New York University, 1972; published New York: Garland Publishing, 1977).

2. John Ruskin, *Seven Lamps of Architecture* (1849; reprint, London: J. M. Dent, 1932), pp. 40, 52. Cropsey met Ruskin in London between 1857 and 1863, and Ruskin occasionally visited Cropsey's studio-house at 2 Kensington Gate, Hyde Park South. One of Cropsey's pocket notebooks, probably dating to 1860, mentions *Stones of Venice*, and it can be conjectured that he was familiar with other works by Ruskin.

3. "Architectural Students—IV," *American Architect and Building News* 1 (Nov. 11, 1876), pp. 362–63.

4. Reginald Blomfield, *Architectural Drawing and Draftsmen* (London: Cassell & Co., 1912), pp. 5–8.

5. Most structures in the 1830s and 1840s were built by skilled artisans with the aid of builders' guides. In the succeeding decades, construction practices were vastly altered by the founding of the American Institute of Architects in 1857; the availability, beginning in 1860, of university level training; technological advances; and the establishment of building codes. See Turpin Bannister, ed., *The Architect at Mid-Century: Evolution and Achievement* (New York: Reinhold Publishing Co., 1954), pp. 93–99.

6. There is no record of their construction in the New York City dockets of new buildings, established, 1866, New York Municipal Archives and Records Center.

7. Cropsey's fascination with city life is expressed in a letter to his fiancée in which he wrote poetically of its visual impact: "Those tall, lean brick buildings that so fertilize our happiness at every sidewalk, looked out of the dusty atmosphere with an air of solemnity. Some light, like burnished gold, tinted an end or a front and not a few chimneys of these parallelogram abodes. The smoke from their chimneys as it wavered upward caught the glowing light and looked red with its intoxication of that bright sunset," J. Cropsey to Maria Cooley, March 30, 1846, coll. Brown Reinhardt, Newark, Del., typescript, NCF. Cropsey maintained active membership in three city clubs: the Century Association, the Union League Club, and the Lotos Club.

8. "Reminiscences of My Own Time" (1846), MS, coll. Brown Reinhardt, Newark, Del., typescript, pp. 4, 5, NCF, microfilm, roll 336, Archives of American Art, Smithsonian Institution, Washington, D.C. This six-page essay, written by Cropsey for C. E. Lester's *Artists in America* (1846), is one of the few source materials on Cropsey's early artistic and architectural development. Henry T. Tuckerman touches briefly on Cropsey's architecture in the *Book of the Artists* (New York: G. P. Putnam & Son, 1867), p. 534.

9. Alexander Jackson Davis, *Rural Residences, Etc., Consisting of Designs, Original and Selected, for Cottages, Villas and Village Churches. . . .* (New York: privately printed, 1837). Davis was also esteemed for his Greek Revival designs.

10. None of Cropsey's architectural drawings executed for Trench appears to have survived. Something of Trench's rising status as an architect may be gleaned from the fact that, although his name was not among the New York architects who met in December of 1836 to help organize the first, short-lived American Institution of Architects, he and his partner John B. Snook (1815–1901) were commissioned less than ten years later to design New York's earliest Italianate commercial palace, the first A. T. Stewart department store, begun in 1845.

11. Cropsey's account book for the year May 1845 to May 1846 lists a payment of five dollars from Trench for drawings. Miscellaneous Letters, Diaries, Sketches, and Memorandums of Jasper Francis Cropsey (cited hereafter as Cropsey Papers), NCF, microfilm, roll 336, Archives of American Art.

12. Cropsey Papers, NCF, microfilm, roll 336, Archives of American Art. John Britton, *The Architectural Antiquities of Great Britain, Represented and Illustrated in a Series of Views, Elevations, Plans, Sections, and Details of Various English Edifices; with Historical and Descriptive Accounts of Each* (London: Longman, Hurst, Rees, and Orme, 1807–27). "Ancient Ecclesiastical Architecture" probably refers to *Cathedral Antiquities, Historical and Decorative Accounts with 311 Illustrations . . . ,* 13 vols. (London: Longman, Hurst, Rees, Orme, and Brown, 1814–31). The pocket journal listing temple forms is in the private collection of James Reinhardt, microfilm at NCF.

13. J. Cropsey to his sister-in-law Jane Cooley (July 2, 1847), coll. Brown Reinhardt, Newark, Del., typescript, NCF.

14. Notebook, Cropsey Papers, NCF, microfilm, roll 337, Archives of American Art. Thomas Rickman, *An Attempt to Discriminate the Styles of Architecture in England*, 5th ed. (London: John Henry Parker, 1848).

15. A statement in Cropsey's hand, dated July 1877, lists outstanding notes totaling $12,591 owed Mr. (or Mrs.) Rutherford, less $3,500 for pictures and architectural services. Cropsey Papers, NCF. The reference is probably to John Rutherford, an art patron who is noted as purchasing a painting of Jedburgh Abbey and, in 1856, *Spirit of War* and *Spirit of Peace*.

16. Deed, Office of the Register, New York City, Cropsey Papers, NCF.

17. Cropsey's use of ciphers as decorative devices may have been an expression of the Ruskinian interest in abstracting designs from medieval manuscripts.

18. *The Architecture of Country Houses; including designs for cottages, farm houses and villas, with remarks on interiors, furniture, and the best modes of warming and ventilating* (New York: D. Appleton & Co., 1866), p. 263.

19. H. Porter to J. Cropsey, Feb. 24, 1874, and March 12, 1874, Cropsey Papers, NCF, microfilm, roll 336, Archives of American Art.

20. Stations were at Rector and New Church streets, Cortlandt and New Church streets, Park Place and Church Street, Chambers Street and West Broadway, Franklin Street, Grand Street and South Fifth Avenue, Bleecker Street, Clinton Place at Greenwich Street and Sixth Avenue, Fourteenth Street and Sixth Avenue, Twenty-third Street, Thirty-third Street, Forty-second Street, Fiftieth Street, and Fifty-eighth Street.

21. "Specifications for Fourteen (14) Double Stations for the Gilbert Elevated Railway Company" (Feb. 1878), Cropsey Papers, NCF, microfilm, roll 905, Archives of American Art.

22. See "Correspondence," *American Architect* 3 (Jan. 26, 1878), p. 33. Among the architects approached for the assignment were Potter and Robertson, C. F. McKim, George Harvey, and A. J. Bloor.

23. "West Side Rapid Transit, The Metropolitan Railway Open," *New York Times* (June 5, 1878), p. 8. The Gilbert Elevated Railway Company had been renamed the Metropolitan Elevated Railway.

24. H. Porter to S. H. Shreve (chief engineer, Cornell Company), Sept. 2, 1878, Cropsey Papers, NCF, refers to the "green tint" of the stations.

25. "Rapid Transit in Earnest. The Gilbert Elevated Railroad," *Frank Leslie's Illustrated Newspaper* 66 (April 27, 1878), pp. 132–34.

26. "Carpenter's Specifications for ½ of the 14th Street Station" (undated), Cropsey Papers, NCF, microfilm, roll 905, Archives of American Art.

27. "Specifications for Gas Fitting" (undated), ibid.

28. "Rapid Transit and Trade; New Channels for Business," *New York Times* (June 18, 1878), p. 8.

29. "Specifications of Painting, and Materials Required in Finishing and Decorating the Drill Room of the 7th Regiment Armory on Lexington Avenue" (undated), Cropsey Papers, NCF, microfilm, roll 905, Archives of American Art.

30. Carrie Rebora in *Jasper Cropsey Watercolors* (New York: National Academy of Design, 1985), p. 19, identifies Webb (1816–99) as a shipbuilder. A member of the National Academy of Design in New York, he could have met Cropsey there.

31. "Jasper F. Cropsey . . . Passes Away at Hastings," *New York Times* (June 23, 1900), p. 7.

PLATES

Side Elevation.

Plate 1: *Side Elevation, Moravian Church, New Dorp, Staten Island*, 1843, watercolor and pencil on paper, 9¼ x 13¾ in. Newington-Cropsey Foundation.

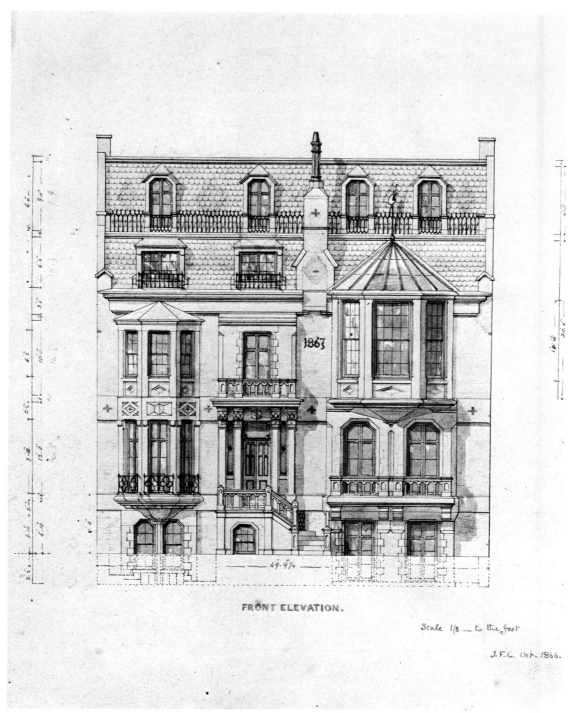

FRONT ELEVATION.

Scale 1/8 — to the foot

J. F. C. Oct. 1866.

Plate 2: *Front Elevation, Town House*, 1866, watercolor and ink on paper, 12½ x 9½ in., signed and dated at lower right: J. F. C. Oct. 1866. Newington-Cropsey Foundation.

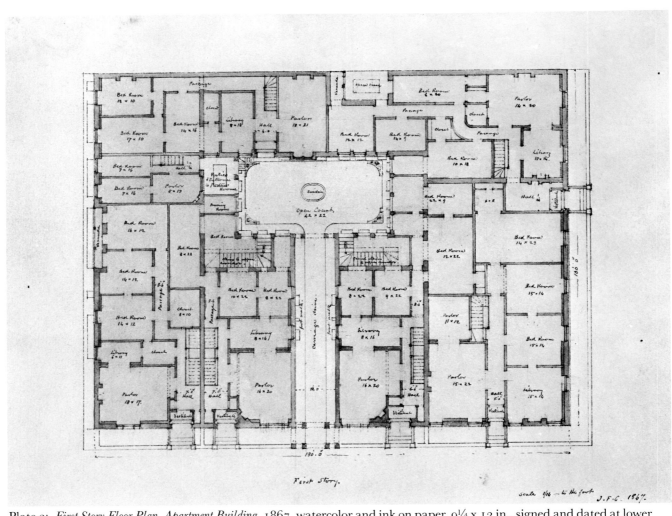

Plate 3: *First Story Floor Plan, Apartment Building*, 1867, watercolor and ink on paper, 9¼ x 12 in., signed and dated at lower right: J. F. C. 1867. Newington-Cropsey Foundation.

Plate 4: *Front Elevation, Row House*, 1871, watercolor and ink on paper, 21¼ x 17 in., signed and dated at lower right: J. F. C. 1871. Newington-Cropsey Foundation.

Plate 5: *Design for Seventh Regiment Armory Drill Hall Decorations*, ca. 1879, watercolor and pencil on paper, 18¼ x 12¾ in., signed at lower left: Cropsey. Newington-Cropsey Foundation.

Plate 6: *Design for Seventh Regiment Armory Drill Hall Decorations*, ca. 1879, watercolor and pencil on paper, 18½ x 12¾ in. Newington-Cropsey Foundation.

Annotated Bibliography of
Jasper F. Cropsey's Library

BY STEPHEN J. ZIETZ

INTRODUCTION

The collection of books in the studio of Jasper F. Cropsey's house in Hastings-on-Hudson, N.Y., represents the remnant of what must once have been a large and significant library. Of the approximately 279 books or sets of books in the studio, 98 have inscriptions that indicate certain ownership by Cropsey, his wife, or their daughters (26 of the 98 are inscribed to Maria or Lilly Cropsey). An additional 112 books, although not inscribed, probably belonged to the Cropsey family. The remainder, approximately 69 books, were almost assuredly added to the collection after Cropsey's death in 1900.

The inscriptions to Cropsey range chronologically from his apprenticeship (1837–42) with the New York architect Joseph Trench to 1900, when Cropsey died. Both of his European stays (1847–49 and 1856–63) are represented, but the majority of inscribed books are from his years in the United States.

Some of Cropsey's books are annotated and others have faint pencil sketches on endpapers. One in particular, C. F. Hoffman's *The Vigil of faith and other poems* (New York, 1842), was embellished by Cropsey with intricate borders in pen and ink on three pages. The theme of these drawings follows that of the poetry: nature and religion.

That the library was large and important, there is no doubt; but it has come down to us in a partial state. Many of the books that Cropsey might have owned—those that reproduced his paintings or for which he provided illustrations (for example, *The Home Book of the Picturesque* and Shinn's *Masterpieces of the Centennial International Exhibition*) and art journals that regularly mentioned him (*Art Journal*, *Crayon*, etc.)—are wanting. Books with engraved plates and lavish illustrations are also not present.

There were at least five sales of Cropsey's personal effects that specifically mentioned books or probably included them. In 1856, before sailing to England, the Cropseys held a sale of paintings and perhaps books; in 1863 a similar sale was held in London before they returned to New York; in 1867 Cropsey's London solicitor sold off the contents of his English house and studio; in 1884 a chattel mortgage sale of the artist's effects was held; and in 1906 there was an auction of Maria Cropsey's estate, which included "a small library of valuable books." Some of the choicest items in the collection may therefore be missing from the extant library.

The books that remain are curiously homogeneous, and they fall into two categories: works supporting the study of natural theology and literary works, mostly poetry, extolling nature or religion. Cropsey

159

was a pious man, and his library confirms his strong religious interests. It contains liturgical works from several Protestant denominations. His religion was compatible with a liberal Protestant type, encompassing a respect for nature as well as traditional religious values. Cropsey's interest in these aspects of nineteenth-century religious thought is clearly reflected in his library as it has come down to us.

BOOKS DEFINITELY BELONGING TO CROPSEY

Alighieri, Dante. *La Divina commedia.* 2a ed. Firenze: Felice Le Monnier, 1843. Inscribed: Maria Cropsey, Rome, 1847.

Alken, Henry. *The Art and practice of etching.* London: S. & J. Fuller, 1849. Inscribed: Jasper F. Cropsey, June 22st. 1849.

Bancroft, George. *Literary and historical miscellanies.* New York: Harper & Brothers, 1855. Inscribed: J. F. Cropsey 1855.

Barrett, William John. *Andreas, a tragedy, in five acts.* London: Thomas Sanderson, 1857. Inscribed: To Jasper Cropsey, with the author's kind regards, 16 Oct. 1857.

Beecher, Henry Ward. *Star papers, or, Experiences of art and nature.* New York: J. C. Derby, 1855. Inscribed: J. F. Cropsey 1855.

Bennett, W. C. *Songs by a song-writer.* London: Chapman & Hall, 1859. Inscribed: J. F. Cropsey, Esq., with all good wishes from W. W. Bennett.

———. *The Worn wedding-ring, and other poems.* London: Chapman and Hall, 1861. Inscribed: J. F. Cropsey, Esq., with all good wishes from Wm. [?] Bennett.

Black's picturesque tourist of Scotland. 5th ed. Edinburgh: Adam and Charles Black, 1847. Inscribed: Mr. J. F. Cropsey, New York, America. Some marginal notes on leaf between map after page 96 and page 97, inscribed: written by Mr. Carr in the carriage, when on my way to York, July 5th, 1847.

Blessington, Marguerite, Countess of, ed. *Heath's book of beauty: 1836.* . . . London: Longman, Rees, Orme, Brown, Green and Longmans, n.d. (1836?). Inscribed: J. F. Cropsey.

The Book of Common Prayer. . . . London: G. E. Eyre and W. Spottiswoode, 1853. Inscribed: Mrs. Maria Cropsey/no. 2 Kensington Gate/Hyde Park, South/London/ 1859 [date in later hand]. (See also p. 164.)

The Bread-winners, a social history. New York: Harper & Brothers, 1884. Inscribed: J. F. Cropsey 1884.

Brougham, John, and John Elderkin, eds. *Lotos leaves.* . . . Boston: William F. Gill and Co., 1875. Inscribed: Jan. 1875, from J. F. Cropsey to Mrs. M. Cropsey.

Browning, Robert. *Poems.* Vol. 2. London: Chapman & Hall, 1849. Inscribed: Maria Cropsey, frm. J. Burrill Custis. (See also p. 164.)

Burnet, John. *The Progress of a painter in the nineteenth century.* . . . London: David Bogue, 1854. Inscribed: J. F. Cropsey from S. P. A. [Samuel Putnam Avery] Bedford, Ano [?] Oct.r/54.

Byron, Lord George. *The works of Lord Byron in verse and prose.* . . . New York: Alex. V. Blake, 1844. Inscribed: J. F. Cropsey Sept. 25 [?], 1845. Some underlining in the poetry section.

Clarkson, L[ida]. *Indian Summer.* . . . New York: E. P. Dutton & Co., 1883. Inscribed: Miss Lilly Cropsey, July 16th, 1883.

Clement Falconer, or, The memoirs of a young Whig. . . . 2 vols. Baltimore: N. Hickman, 1838. Vol. 1 inscribed: Jasper F. Cropsey, New York—1838. Vol. 2 inscribed: Jasper F. Cropsey, New York 1838. Pseudonyms are used throughout the text. Cropsey has penciled in the real names.

The Cottage Bible and family expositor. . . . Hartford: D. F. Robinson and H. F. Sumner, 1834. 2 vols. Inscribed: J. F. Cropsey, 157 Franklin St., New York, Presented to me by my Father [small pencil sketch of foliage] subjects 1. Garden of Eden, The expulsion, Emnitids [?] on Isac & Rebecca. Also inscribed: subjects, The staying up of Moses' wand [. . . ?], Jehova [. . . ?] The Lord is my [. . . ?] Exodus 17: 8–15. On next leaf: small figure sketches. Last front endpaper: two small landscape sketches. Volume 2 has "family record." Faint pencil sketch on inside of back cover.

Cronin, David E. [Major Seth Eyland, pseud.] *The Evolution of a life / described in the memoirs of Major Seth Eyland*. New York: S. W. Green's Son, 1884. Inscribed: To J. F. Cropsey, N.A.—with compliments of the author David E. Cronin. 206 Broadway, Room 88, N.Y. Jan.y 20th, '85. Chapter 6, p. 63, refers to Cropsey. Beginning of page 74: "I had heard that Mr. Cropsey, the American artist, was residing in London. . . ."

[Curtis, George William]. *Nile notes of A. Howadji*. New York: Harper & Brothers, 1851. Inscribed: Mrs. Cropsey—with regards of J. Burrill Custis—1851—.

Daily light on the daily path. . . . London: Samuel Bagster & Sons, n.d. Space left throughout for calendar entries. Inscribed in this copy: Dec. 28, Jennie born 1852; Aug. 6, Rose died 1892, Constance born 1879; Aug. 27, Mamma born 1829; Sept. 5, Minnie born 1850; Feb. 18, Papa borm [*sic*] 1823; Feb. 21, Dear Lilly died at 9½ a.m. 1889; March 28, Dear Mamma died at 12 a.m. 1906; Feb. 25, Rose born 1858; May 1, Mamma married 1847; June 22, Dear Papa died, at 9 a.m. 1900; July 16, Lilly born 1859.

De Stael, Madame. *Corinne, ou, L'Italie*. Nouvelle ed., precedée d'une notice par Mme. Necker de Saussine. Paris: Charpentier, 1843. Inscribed: Maria Cropsey, Rome, 1847.

The Devotional family Bible. . . . Commentary by Alexander Fletcher. 2 vols. London & New York: George Virtue, n.d. Bookplate indicates it was Cropsey's in 1855. Volume 1 inscribed: To Lawrence Cortelyou Smith from his great-grand mother Maria Cropsey, "Everest," Hastings-on-Hudson, August twenty nine nineteen hundred six.

Drake, Joseph Rodman. *The Culprit Fay*. New York: Rudd & Carleton, 1859. Inscribed: To Friend Cropsey from S. P. A. [Samuel Putnam Avery] N.Y. 1859. (See also p. 165.)

Eastlake, Charles Lock. *Materials for a history of oil painting*. London: Longman, Brown, Green, and Longmans, 1847. Signed: Jasper F. Cropsey Rome, Jan.y 13th., 1848.

[Eaton, Charlotte]. *Rome, in the nineteenth century*. . . . 2nd ed. Edinburgh: James Ballantyne and Co., for Archibald Constable and Co., 1822. 3 vols., all 3 inscribed: Jasper F. Cropsey. Vol. 2 has figure sketches on first front free endpaper (man and woman, man in armor). Vol. 1 has full-page pencil landscape sketch on last free endpaper.

Edwards, Rev. Justin. *The Sabbath manual*. . . . New York: American Tract Society, n.d. Inscribed: Mariah Cropsey.

Fairholt, F. W. *Costume in England: a history of dress from the earliest period till the close of the eighteenth century*. . . . London: Chapman and Hall, 1846. Inscribed: J. F. Cropsey 1852. The chapters on the fourteenth and fifteenth centuries have several small annotations.

Farrar, Frederic W. *The Life of Christ*. New York: E. P. Dutton & Co. (1890?). Inscribed: Mr. + Mrs. Jasper F. Cropsey, Kalonduia [?] Hastings on Hudson, New York, with kindest regards + in memory of a very pleasant day spent at this lovely house, J. Boyd. Dated at top in pencil: June 1891.

Field, Henry M. *Summer pictures: from Copenhagen to Venice*. New York: Sheldon & Co., 1859. Inscribed: Mrs. J. F. Cropsey, with the affectionate regards of her friend, H. M. Field, New York, May 25, 1859.

Gibbon, Edward. *The History of the decline and fall of the Roman Empire*. Abridged by the Rev. Charles Hereford. Halifax: William Milner, 1846. Underlining throughout. On recto of last free endpaper: landscape sketches (rocks, etc.), one of which has been cancelled.

Goldsmith, Oliver. *The works of Oliver Goldsmith*. . . . With introduction, notes, and a life of Oliver Goldsmith by John Francis Waller. London: Cassell, Peller, and Galpin, n.d. Inscribed: J. F. Cropsey. Frontispiece is glued to endpaper, hiding inscription in ink.

Goodrich, A. G., ed. *The Token and Atlantic souvenir*. . . . Boston: Charles Bowen, 1836. Inscribed: J. F. Cropsey.

The Guide of Rome and the environs according to Vasi and Nibby. . . . 3rd ed. Rome: L. Piale, 1847. Inscribed: Mr. Jasper F. Cropsey, Rome, Oct. 7th, 1847.

Guide to Naples and Sicily. Rome: L. Piale, 1847. Inscribed: J. F. Cropsey, Naples, August, 1847. On verso of front free endpaper: landscape sketch with color notations. On last free endpaper: another small landscape sketch.

Hall, S. C., ed. *The Book of gems: the modern poets and artists of Great Britain*. 3 vols. London: Whittaker and Co., 1836–38. Inscribed: J. F. Cropsey 1854.

———. *An Old story*. London: Virtue, Spalding and Co., n.d. (after 1872). Inscribed: To my valued friend, Jasper F. Cropsey, New York FAK—Kensington.

Hand-book for travellers in France. . . . 3rd ed. London: John Murray, 1848. Inscribed: Jasper F. Cropsey.

Hand-book for travellers in Northern Italy. . . . 3rd ed. London: John Murray, 1847. Inscribed: Jasper F. Cropsey / Hotel de [*sic*] Nord.

Hawthorne, Nathaniel. *Twice-told tales.* Vol. 1. Boston: James Munroe and Co., 1845. Inscribed: Maria Cooley.

Hayne, Paul H. *The Mountain of the lovers.* . . . New York: E. J. Hale & Son, 1875. Inscribed: J. F. Cropsey Esq, with regards of Gersp [. . . ?] Perry, Warwick, 29th Sept. 75 [?].

Hayter, Charles. *An Introduction to perspective, practical geometry, drawing and painting.* . . . 6th ed. London: Samuel Bagster and Sons, 1845. Inscribed: J. F. Cropsey 1854.

Hemans, Felicia. *Poems.* Philadelphia: John Ball, 1849. Inscribed: Mrs. Maria Cropsey with affectionate regards of E. M. G.

Hill, G. *The Ruins of Athens; Titania's Banquet, a mask; and other poems.* Boston: Otis, Broaders & Co., 1839. Inscribed: J. F. Cropsey April 26, 1845.

Hillard, George Stillman. *Six months in Italy.* 4th ed. Vol. 1. Boston: Ticknor, Reed, and Fields, 1854. Inscribed: Mrs. Cropsey from her friend H. S.

Hoffman, C. F. *The Vigil of faith and other poems.* New York: S. Colman, 1842. Pages 5, 7, and 9 have decorative borders drawn with pen and ink. Page 5, above: angel, pointing to anchor of faith; below: canoe under tree. Page 7: landscape, partially ruined. Page 9: waterfall, boat, and sunset.

Hope, Thomas. *Costumes of the ancients.* New ed. London: Henry G. Bohn, 1841. Inscribed: J. F. Cropsey, New York.

Howard, Frank. *The Science of drawing, being a progressive series of the characteristic forms of nature.* . . . London: William Pickering, 1839. Vol. 1 — *Trees.* Vol. 3 — *The Human Form.* Vol. 3 inscribed: J. F. Cropsey, 1847.

Howells, William D. *A Modern instance, a novel.* Boston: James R. Osgood and Co., 1822. Inscribed: J. F. Cropsey 1885.

Hunt, Leigh. *The Old court suburb, or, Memorials of Kensington.* . . . 2 vols. London: Hurst and Blackett, 1855. Vol. 1 inscribed: J. F. Cropsey. Vol. 2 inscribed: J. F. Cropsey, London, Oct. 7th, 1856.

Hutcheson, John Conroy. *The Pettyshams, a novel.* . . . Vol. 1. London: T. Cautley Newby, 1867. Inscribed: Mrs. Cropsey with the author's compts. (See also p. 165.)

Jarves, James Jackson. *Art-hints: architecture, sculpture, and painting.* New York: Harper & Brothers, 1855. Inscribed: J. F. Cropsey 1855. Many marginal notes, including: p. 144, "If nature is so much superior to art, why should he attempt to improve her beauties?"; p. 290, "*Prow* of the boat" corrects the use in text of "stern" in discussion of Leutze's *Washington Crossing the Delaware;* p. 294, "Alluding I suppose to the Pre-Raphlete [*sic*] School" about mention of a "new era in art"; p. 299, about Joseph Vernet's drawing well but lacking gift of color, "quite to the contrary"; p. 301, "The Author seems to have strange ideas of transparency all though the book. He seems to think every thing should look like glass"; p. 307, when text refers to the genius of an Allston which would have distinguished even the old world, Cropsey added, "and where is *Cole* Stuart too."

Keats, John. *The Eve of St. Agnes.* New York: D. Appleton & Co., 1856. Inscribed: M. Cropsey, from H. M., Jan.y 6 '56.

Knight, Charles, ed. *The Pictorial edition of the works of Shakespeare.* Vol. 1. London: Charles Knight and Co., n.d. Inscribed: J. F. Cropsey Sept 1850.

Knight, Rev. James. *A Concise treatise on the truth and importance of the Christian religion.* . . . London: Longman & Co., 1856. Inscribed: J. F. Cropsey, Esq.

Legislative manual of the State of New-York, 1834. Albany: Croswell, Van Benthuysen and Burt, 1834. Inscribed: Jasper F. Cropsey.

Leslie, C. R. *Memoirs of the life of John Constable, Esq. R.A.: composed chiefly of his letters.* 2nd ed. London: Longman, Brown, Green and Longmans, 1845. Inscribed: To J. F. Cropsey, from his Friend, S. P. Avery, Dec. 1853.

Lindsay, Lord. *Sketches of the history of Christian art.* 3 vols. London: John Murray, 1847. All 3 vols. inscribed: Jasper F. Cropsey, June 25th, 1849. Vol. 1, on last free endpaper: This city aila [?] — near the Red Sea — mentioned by Dr. Robinson — "Researches in Palestine." In Vol. 2, between pages 232 and 233 on one side of folded green paper: Volume 1 — It Hilarion — Journal to Bethulia — page 129 + 30 Saw Antony / Babylon, over the cite [*sic*] of which the modern Cairo extends / Bistre + yellow colours of [. . . much more]. Notes on the appearance of Jesus.

London, Mrs. *Botany for ladies, or, A popular introduction to the natural system of plants.* . . . London: John Murray,

1842. Inscribed: Mrs. J. F. Cropsey, with regards of J. M. Falconer, 15 May 1847. Sketches in pencil on back endpaper, one signed: J. F. Cropsey May 28 1847.

Longfellow, Henry Wadsworth. *The Seaside and the fireside.* Boston: Ticknor, Reed, and Fields, 1850. Inscribed: Maria Cropsey, 1852.

Lyell, Sir Charles. *Principles of geology, or, The modern changes of the earth and its inhabitants considered as illustrative of geology.* 9th ed. Inscribed: J. F. Cropsey, 1854.

Mackay, Charles. *The Salamandrine.* London: Ingram, Cooke, and Co., 1853. Inscribed: J. F. Cropsey, 1852.

———, ed. *Songs of England.* . . . London: Houlston & Wright, n.d. Inscribed: J. F. Cropsey.

Meadows, F. C. *New Italian and English dictionary in two parts.* . . . 8th ed. London: William Tegg & Co., 1848. Faint pencil landscape sketch on first front free endpaper.

Medhurst, Mrs. *Garden fables, or, Flowers of speech.* London: Saunders, Otley and Co., 1861. Inscribed: Maria Cropsey, London, 1865.

Miller, Thomas. *Poems.* New ed. London: Chapman and Hall, 1848. Inscribed: Mrs. J. F. Cropsey.

Munter, Balthasar. *G.-F. Struenzee, biografia religiosa.* Firenze: Tip. Le Monnier, 1848. Inscribed: Maria Cropsey / [a verse in French] / T. P. Rome, Janvier 1849.

The New Testament of Our Lord and Saviour Jesus Christ. . . . New York: American Bible Society, 1871. Inscribed: Mrs. [?] Jasper F. Cropsey, New York 1872.

Noble, Louis L. *The Lady Angeline, a lay of the Appalachians.* . . . New York: Sheldon, Blakeman & Co., 1856. Inscribed: J. F. Cropsey, with regards of J. N. Paleroy [?] New York Oct. [?] 27/56.

Oldmixon, Capt. [John W.] *Transatlantic wanderings, or, A last look at the United States.* London: Geo. Routledge & Co., 1855. Inscribed: J. F. Cropsey, London, 1855.

Palmer, J. C. *Thulia.* . . . New York: Samuel Colman, 1843. Inscribed: Comp.mts of John P. Ridner to Miss Maria Cooley, Westmilford, N.J., 1845.

Parmly, Eleazar. *Thoughts in rhyme.* New York: Thomas Holman, 1867. Inscribed: For, Mr. & Mrs. Cropsey with high respect, and friendly regard from E. Parmly, New York, 28th December 1867.

Phillips, Samuel. *Guide to the Crystal Palace and park* and *The Portrait Gallery of the Crystal Palace,* bound together.

London: Crystal Palace Library and Bradbury and Evans, 1856 and 1854, respectively. Inscribed: J. F. Cropsey Sept. 3rd 1856. On verso of back free endpaper are travel and shopping notes.

Richards, William C., ed. *The Shak[e]speare calendar, or, Wit and Wisdom for every day in the year.* New York: George P. Putnam, 1850. Inscribed: To Mrs. Cropsey, with respects of T. Addison Richards 1850.

Rickman, Thomas. *An attempt to discriminate the styles of architecture in England, from the Conquest to the Reformation.* . . . 5th ed. London: John Henry Parker, 1848. Inscribed: J. F. Cropsey.

Rogers, Samuel. *Italy, a poem.* London: Edward Moxon, 1842. Inscribed: J. F. Cropsey 1854.

———. *Poems.* London: Edward Moxon, 1842. Inscribed: J. F. Cropsey 1854.

Stoddard, Richard Henry. *Poems.* Inscribed: Mrs. J. F. Cropsey from S. P. A. [Samuel Putnam Avery].

Talfourd, T. N. *Tragedies: to which are added a few sonnets and verses.* New York: C. S. Francis & Co., 1849. Inscribed: Mr. J. F. Cropsey, from his friend H. P. Tappan.

Tappan, Henry P. *Elements of logic.* . . . New York: D. Appleton and Co., 1856. Inscribed: Mr. J. F. Cropsey from his friend the Author, Jan. 1856.

Tennyson, Alfred. *Maud, and other poems.* Boston: Ticknor and Fields, 1855. Inscribed: J. F. Cropsey 1855.

———. *Maud and other poems.* London: Edward Moxon, 1855. Inscribed: J. F. Cropsey, 1857. Some verses pointed out in pencil.

———. *Poems.* 2 vols. 4th ed. London: Edward Moxon, 1846. Both volumes inscribed: Maria Cropsey f.m her friend J. Burrill Custis, July 22, 1849.

Thenot, Jean Pierre. *Practical perspective: for the use of students.* Translated from the French by one of Thenot's pupils. New York: William Jackson, 1838. Inscribed: Jasper F. Cropsy [sic] New York Oct. 27th 1842. Sketches on verso of first front free endpaper and recto of second front free endpaper.

Thomas, Mrs. Edward. *Autumnal leaves.* . . . London: W. Walker and Co., 1860. Inscribed: Mr[s?] Cropsey with the kind regards of the Authoress.

Train, George Francis. *Spread-eagleism.* London: Sampson Low, Son, & Co., 1860. Inscribed: With the author's compliments.

——— . *Young America abroad in Europe, Asia, and Australia*. . . . London: Sampson Low, Son, & Co., 1857. Inscribed: With the author's compliments to J. F. Cropsey 1857.

Tuckerman, Henry T. *A Memorial of Horatio Greenough*. . . . New York: G. P. Putnam & Co., 1853. Inscribed: J. F. Cropsey.

Tupper, Martin Farquhar. *Proverbial philosophy*. . . . New York: Wiley & Putnam, 1846. Inscribed: Miss Maria Cooley, from J. A. R., New York, July 3rd, 1846. (See also p. 168.)

Vinet, A[lexandre]. *Chrestomathie française, ou, Choix de morceaux tirés des meilleurs écrivains français*. . . . 3e ed. Bruxelles: Meline, Cans et cie., 1838. Inscribed: Jasper F. Cropsey, Rome, 1848, [?]'s tomb at Avignon, April 29th 1849.

Weale, John, ed. *London exhibited in 1851: elucidating its natural and physical characteristics*. . . . London: J. Weale (1851?). Inscribed over earlier, erased inscription: Jasper F. Cropsey, 1851.

Webster, Noah. *A Dictionary of the English language*. . . . Revised and enlarged by Chauncey A. Goodrich. London: David Bogue, 1856. Inscribed: J. F. Cropsey, Aug. 27, 1858.

Webster's Royal red book, or, Court and fashionable register for January, 1862. . . . London: W. & A. Webster (1862?). Page 332: Cropsey, Jasper F. Esq. 2 Kensington-gate, W. (Other names and addresses are listed, probably not by Cropsey.)

Willis, N. Parker, ed. *Trenton Falls, picturesque and descriptive*. New York: George P. Putnam, 1851. Inscribed: J. F. Cropsey.

Wood, Alphonso. *A Class-book of botany: designed for colleges, academies, and other seminaries where science is taught*. . . . Boston: Crocker & Brewster, 1845. Inscribed: J. F. Cropsey, Sept. 9th 1846—. P. 4 of Tables and p. 22 of Flora are annotated with corrections.

Cropsey's Sketching Portfolio. Contains pen and ink sketch for Century Twelfth Night 1899 invitation; printed Kit-Kat Smoker 1898 invitation (illustration not by Cropsey); undated pen and ink invitation to Twelfth Night exhibition at the Century; printed invitation for J. H. Dolph and Hamilton 1892 exhibition; article entitled "American etchers" reprinted in 1886 by Frederick Keppel & Co. from the *Century Magazine* for February 1883; *Catalogue of the New York*

Etching Club exhibition . . . held at the National Academy of Design, New York, 1885. Interior of the portfolio spine is labeled: J. F. Cropsey Hastings-on-Hudson, N.Y. 1886.

Books Probably Belonging to Cropsey

Ackermans Forgetmenot 1847

Aikin, Berkeley. *The Dean, or, The Popular preacher, a tale*. 3 vols. London: Saunders, Otley and Co., 1859. Inscribed: With the author's compts.

Annual report of the State Engineer and Surveyor on the New York State canals: for the fiscal year ending September 30, 1876. Albany: Jerome B. Parmenter, 1877.

Apgar, Austin C. *Trees of the Northern United States*. . . . New York: American Book Co., 1892.

Artists' Fund Society. *Constitution and first [–10th] annual report of the Artists' Fund Society of the City of New York, 1861 [–1869/70]*. New York: G. A. Whitehorne, 1861–1870. Cropsey's name does not appear as a member until the fourth report, 1864, in which he is listed as a member-elect. Thereafter he is a member; in 1865/66 and 1866/67 he served on the Committee on Admissions.

Balzac, Honoré de. *Eugenie Grandet*. Translated by Ellen Marriage. New York: F. M. Lupton Pub. Co., n.d. Dedicated to Maria, on verso of title page is mounted a chromolithograph portrait watercolored over, with "Maria" written beneath.

Beamish, Richard. *Memoir of the life of Sir Marc Isambard Brunel*. . . . London: Longman, Green, Longman and Roberts, 1862. Ex-library copy: Bristol Free Libraries, Redland District, withdrawn.

Bible: The Holy Bible. . . . Oxford: At the University Press, 1861.

The Bijou, an annual of literature and the arts. London: William Pickering . . . , 1829.

The Book of Common Prayer. . . . London: William Collins, 1858. (See also p. 160.)

Browning, Robert. *Poems*. New ed. London: Chapman & Hull, 1849. (See also p. 160.)

Bryant, William Cullen. *Poems by William Cullen Bryant.* . . . London: Sampson Low, Son, & Co., 1858.

Campbell, Thomas. *The Poetical Works of Thomas Campbell.* . . . 2 vols. London: Henry Colburn and Richard Bentley, 1830. Title page inscribed: Robert Austin.

Century Association. *Reports, constitution, by-laws and list of members of the Century Association: for the year[s] 1890 [1896 and 1898].* New York: The Association, 1891 [1897 and 1899]. Cropsey listed as member.

——— . *Reports, constitution, by-laws and list of members of The Century Association, for the year[s] 1891[–1899].* 6 vols. New York, 1892–1900. Cropsey is listed as member in all the volumes present; obituaries of members are given, and it is to be assumed that Cropsey's would have appeared in the next year.

Chalmers, Rev. Thomas. *Discourses on the Christian revelation viewed in connexion with the modern astronomy.* Andover: Mark Newman, 1818.

Christman, Rev. Henry, ed. *The Poetical remains of Peter John Allan, Esq.* . . . London: Smith, Elder, & Co., 1853.

Comical creatures: a picture book for the nursery. . . . London: T. Nelson and Sons . . . , 1868. Child's scribblings on several pages.

Cooper, James Fenimore. *The Deerslayer, a tale.* New York: F. M. Lupton Pub. Co., n.d.

——— . *The Last of the Mohicans.* . . . 2 vols., 4th ed. Philadelphia: H. C. Carey & I. Lee, 1834.

Dana, Richard Henry. *To Cuba and back.* . . . Boston: Ticknor and Fields, 1859.

Drake, Joseph Rodman. *The Culprit Fay, and other poems.* New York: Van Norden and King, 1847. (See also p. 161.)

Eaton, Daniel Cady. *Beautiful Ferns.* From the original watercolor drawings after nature by C. E. Faxon and J. H. Emerton, descriptive text by Daniel Cady Eaton. Boston: S. E. Cassino, 1882.

Family Bible, the New Testament of Our Lord and Saviour Jesus Christ. With notes and instructions by Rev. Justin Edwards. New York: American Tract Society, 1851.

Foster, Birket. *Birket Foster's pictures of English landscape.* Engraved by the Brothers Dalziel, pictures in words by Tom Taylor. London: Routledge, Warne, and Routledge, 1863.

French lesson book (title page missing). Preface dated: Brooklyn, 1869.

Galignani's new Paris guide. Paris: A. and W. Galignani and Co., 1847.

Gallenga, Antonio. *Country life in Piedmont.* London: Chapman and Hall, 1858.

Gardiner, William. *Twenty lessons on British mosses, or, First steps to a knowledge of that beautiful tribe of plants.* 2nd ed. Edinburgh: David Mathers, 1846.

Gautier, Theophile. *Wanderings in Spain.* London: Ingram, Cooke, and Co., 1853.

Gray, Asa. *First lessons in botany and vegetable physiology.* . . . New York: G. P. Putnam & Co. and Ivison & Phinney, 1857.

Gray, Thomas. *An Elegy written in a country churchyard.* New York: D. Appleton and Co., 1854.

The Habits of good society: a handbook for ladies and gentlemen. From the last London ed. New York: Carleton, 1866.

Hall, S. C., ed. *The Amulet.* London: Frederick Westley and A. H. Davis, 1835.

Harris, Amanda B. *Wild flowers and where they grow.* Boston: D. Lothrop and Co., 1882.

Havernagel, Frances Ridley. *Morning stars.* New York: Anson D. F. Randolph & Co., n.d. Inscribed: Isabel Amelia Wack, Hastings-upon-Hudson, N.Y. Sunday, March 11–189[1, 4, or 7].

Hayward, A. *The Art of dining, or, Gastronomy and gastronomers.* New ed. London: John Murray, 1883.

Hutcheson, John Conroy. *The Pettyshams, a novel.* . . . Vol. 2. London: T. Cautley Newby, 1867. (See also p. 162.)

Irving, Washington. *The Works of Washington Irving.* 21 vols. New ed., revised. New York: Geo. P. Putnam, 1860–61.

James, M. E. *How to decorate our ceilings, walls, and floors.* London: George Bell & Sons, 1883.

Jenkyn, Thomas W. *On the extent of the atonement, in relation to God and the universe.* From the London ed. Boston: Crocker and Brewster . . . , 1835.

Johns, Rev. C. A. *The Forest trees of Britain.* 2nd ed. 2 vols. London: Society for Promoting Christian Knowledge, 1849.

——— , ed. *Gardening for children.* 2nd ed. London: Charles Cox. Preface dated: 1849. Calling card engraved "Mr. W. Holman Hunt" between pages 18 and 19.

Juvenile forget-me-not for 1837. London: F. Westley and A. H. Davis, 1837.

Kirkland, Mrs. C[aroline] M. *Western clearings.* London: Wiley & Putnam, 1846.

Lacroix, Paul. *Les arts au Moyen Age et à l'époque de la Renaissance.* 5eme ed. Paris: Firmin Didot Frères, fils et cie., 1874.

———. *XVIII siècle: institutions, usages et costumes. . . .* 3eme ed. Paris: Firmin-Didot et cie., 1878.

———. *XVIII siècle: lettres, sciences et arts. . . .* 2eme ed. Paris: Firmin-Didot et cie., 1878.

———. *XVII siècle: institutions, usage et costumes. . . .* Paris: Firmin-Didot et cie., 1880.

———. *Sciences & lettres au Moyen Age et à l'époque de la Renaissance.* 3eme ed. Paris: Firmin-Didot et cie., 1876.

———. *Sciences et lettres au Moyen Age et à l'époque de la Renaissance.* Paris: Firmin-Didot et cie., 1877.

———. *Vie militaire et religieuse au Moyen Age et à l'époque de la Renaissance.* 3eme ed. Paris: Firmin-Didot et cie., 1876.

The Landscape annual. 8 vols. London: R. Jennings, 1830–35, 1838–39.

Lauder, Sir Thomas Dick. *Sir Uvedale Price on the picturesque. . . .* Edinburgh: Caldwell, Lloyd and Co., 1842.

The Law of art copyright. . . . Introduction and notes by E. M. Underdown. London: John Crockford, 1863.

Lennie, William. *The Principles of English grammar. . . .* 44th ed. Edinburgh: Oliver & Boyd, 1858.

The life of a tree. London: Society for Promoting Christian Knowledge, 1849.

Lindsay, Lord. *Letters on Egypt, Edom and the Holy Land.* 4th ed. London: Henry Colburn, 1847.

Lowell, James Russell. *Fireside travels.* London: Macmillan and Co., 1864.

Lyell, Sir Charles. *A Manual of elementary geology, or, The Ancient changes of the earth and its inhabitants as illustrated by geological monuments.* 4th ed. London: John Murray, 1852. Pages uncut, indicating that the book was never read.

Lytton, Lord Edward George. *The Dramatic works of the Right Hon. Lord Lytton.* London & New York: George Routledge and Sons, n.d. Newspaper clipping from *World*, Aug. 24, 1884, glued to inside of back cover.

Macaulay, Thomas Babington. *Lays of Ancient Rome.* Philadelphia: E. H. Butler & Co., 1853.

[Mantell, Gideon Algernon]. *Thoughts on a pebble, or, A first lesson in geology.* 8th ed. London: Reeve, Benham, and Reeve, 1849.

Marcy, E. E. *Christianity and its conflicts, ancient and modern.* New York: D. Appleton and Co., 1867.

Markham, Mrs. *A History of France. . . .* New and revised ed. London: John Murray, 1859. Inscribed: Lilly. Many woodcuts watercolored.

Mavor, William. *The English spelling-book. . . .* New ed. London: P. MacDonald, 1861.

Mills, Abraham. *Lectures on rhetoric and belles lettres: chiefly from the lectures of Dr. Blair.* New ed. New York: Roe Lockwood, 1842.

Mitchell, Donald Grant [Ik Marvel, pseud.]. *Dream-life, a fable of the seasons.* Philadelphia: Henry Altemus, 1895. Inscribed: Isabel—wishing you a merry Xmas. Palmer 12/25/95.

Moore, Thomas. *The Epicurean, a tale.* With vignette illustrations by J. M. W. Turner . . . and Alciphron, a poem, by Thomas Moore. . . . London: John Macrone, 1839.

[Moquin-Tandon, Christian Horace B. A.] *The World of the sea.* Translated and enlarged by the Rev. H. Martyn Hart, M.A., from *Le Monde de la mer* by Mons. Moquin-Tandon. London: Cassell, Petter, and Galpin (ca. 1869).

National Academy of Design. *National Academy notes and complete catalogue: sixty-first Spring exhibition, National Academy of Design, New York. . . .* Charles M. Kurtz, ed. New York: Cassell & Co., 1886. Cropsey listed as academician (1851). Cropsey showed in Corridor, no. 54, *October on the Hudson* (for sale for $500), illustrated p. 116; East Gallery, no. 363, *A Glimpse of the River* ($350); South Gallery, no. 588, *Autumn, Lake George* ($85); North-west Gallery, no. 777, *A Showery Day* ($275); West Gallery, no. 704, *Hudson River, From the Old Quarry, Hastings* ($350).

O'Connor, William D. *The Ghost.* New York: G. P. Putnam & Son, 1867.

Oldmixon, John. *Gleanings from Piccadilly to Pera.* London: Longman, Brown, Green and Longmans, 1854.

[Paget, Francis Edward]. *The Owlet of Owlstone Edge.* 4th ed. London: Joseph Masters, 1858.

Pratt, Anne. *The green fields and their grasses.* London: Society for Promoting Christian Knowledge, 1852.

Priced catalogue of artist's materials: supplies for oil and water color painting, pastel and miniature painting. . . . New York: F. W. Devoe & Co. (ca. 1878).

Proctor, Richard A. *Other worlds than ours.* New York: P. F. Collier & Son. Preface dated: 1870.

[Reformed Church in America]. *Psalms and hymns, with the doctrinal standards and liturgy, of the Reformed Church in America.* New York: Board of Publications (ca. 1859).

———. *The Psalms and hymns . . . of the Synod of Dort, and liturgy of the Reformed Protestant Dutch Church in North America.* Philadelphia: William G. Mentz, 1854.

Richards, T. Addison. *Romance of American landscape.* New York: Leavitt & Allen, 1855.

Richardson, C. J. *The Englishman's house, from a cottage to a mansion.* . . . 2nd ed. London: John Camden Hotten (ca. 1871?).

[Ritchie, Leitch]. *The Rivers of France from drawings by J. M. W. Turner.* London: Longman, Rees, Orme, Brown, Green & Longman, 1837.

Roberts, M. E. [Mrs. Nemo, pseud.] *A Series of appeals, or, Lectures addressed not behind a curtain to one unfortunate man, but to all men and their families.* Albany: J. Munsell, 1863.

Roche, M. A. *Les Prosateurs français.* . . . 5eme ed. London: Dulau et cie., 1856.

Rollin, Charles. *The Ancient history of the Egyptians, Carthaginians, Assyrians, Babylonians, Medes and Persians, Grecians, and Macedonians.* . . . 2 vols. 1st complete American ed. New York: Harper & Brothers, 1839.

[Ruskin, John]. *Pre-Raphaelitism* and *Notes on the construction of sheepfolds* (2nd ed.), bound together. London: Smith, Elder, and Co., 1851.

Scott, Sir Walter. *The Abbot, being a sequel to the Monastery.* (Waverly novels, pocket ed., vol. 11) New York: Scribner, Welford & Armstrong, 1873.

———. *The Lady of the Lake.* New York & London: F. A. Stokes, 1895. Inscribed: To Miss Isabel Wack, wishing you a Merry Xmas—1897, Wilfrid Nouggins [?].

———. *The Monastery.* (Waverly novels, pocket ed., vol. 10) New York: Scribner, Welford & Armstrong, 1873.

———. *The Poetical Works of Sir Walter Scott.* New York: D. Appleton and Co., 1850.

Selby, Prideaux John. *A History of British forest-trees, indigenous and introduced.* London: John Van Vorst, 1842.

Shaw, Thomas B. *Outlines of English literature.* Philadelphia: Lea and Blanchard, 1849.

[Shee, Martin Archer]. [*Rhymes on art, or, The Remonstrance, &c.*] (title page missing). Preface dated: 1805. Pagination: lxvii, (3), 4–130 p.: 16 cm.

Sheldon, G. W. *American Painters.* . . . New York: D. Appleton and Co., 1878. Errors in the Cropsey biography, p. 82, have been corrected by hand.

Sketches from Venetian history. Vol. 2. New York: Harper & Brothers, 1839.

[Smith, Rev. Sydney]. *The Wit and wisdom of the Rev. Sydney Smith.* . . . London: Longman, Green, Longman, and Roberts, 1860.

Smith, William. *A Small classical dictionary of biography, mythology, and geography.* . . . New ed. London: John Murray, 1853.

Snelling, Mrs. Anna L. *Kabaosa, or, The warriors of the West, a tale of the last war.* New York: Printed for the publisher by D. Adee, 1842.

Stafford, Robert. *Enoch, a poem in three books.* 2nd ed. London: Longman, Green, Longman & Roberts, 1860.

Stedman, Edmund Clarence, and Ellen Mackay Hutchinson, eds. [*Prospectus for*] *A Library of American literature from the earliest settlement to the present time.* New York: Charles L. Webster & Co., 1891.

Symington, Andrew James. *The Beautiful in nature, art, and life.* Longman, Brown, Green and Longmans and Roberts, 1857. Pages are largely uncut, indicating that the book was probably unread.

Tatlor, W. C. *A Manual of ancient and modern history.* . . . Revised, with a chapter on the history of the United States, by C. S. Henry. 11th ed. New York: D. Appleton & Co., 1867.

Taylor, W. B. Sarsfield. *The Origin, progress and present condition of the fine arts in Great Britain and Ireland.* 2 vols. London: Whittaker & Co., 1841.

Tennyson, Alfred. *Enoch Arden.* Boston: Ticknor and Fields, 1865.

Timbs, John. *School-days of eminent men.* . . . New ed. London: Lockwood and Co. (ca. 1860s).

Toulmin, Camilla. *Lays and Legends, illustrative of English life*. London: Jeremiah How, 1845.

[Tupper, Martin F.] *Proverbial philosophy, a book of thoughts and arguments, originally treated by Martin Farquhar Tupper.* First and second series: 3rd American, from the 5th London ed. Philadelphia: Herman Hooker, 1846. (See also p. 164.)

Webb, Laura S. *Custer's immortality, a poem. . . .* New York: Evening Post Stream Presses (1876?). Inscribed: To Lilly in the Valley of the Shadow of Death. . . . From her unknown friend Laura S. Webb, N.Y. Oct. 27th 1876.

Willmott, Rev. Robert Aris, ed. *The Poets of the nineteenth century.* London: George Routledge & Co., 1857.

Chronology

1823	Jasper F. Cropsey was born on February 18th in Rossville, Staten Island.
1837	His model of a country house won him a diploma at the Mechanics' Institute Fair.
1837–1842	Worked as an apprentice in the office of the New York architect Joseph Trench. Studied watercolor with Edward Maury. Made first oil paintings, using Trench's office as a studio.
1843	Exhibited for the first time at the National Academy of Design (*Landscape Composition*, 1843, no. 155). Established his own architectural practice at 72 Chambers Street in New York.
1844	Was elected an associate of the National Academy of Design for his painting *View in Orange County with Greenwood Lake in the Distance*, 1844 (no. 68).
1847	In May, he married Maria Cooley of West Milford, New Jersey, and they sailed for England. Left England for Italy in September. By mid-October, settled into Thomas Cole's former studio in Rome.
1848	Visited the coast of southern Italy during the summer. His friends included the artists Christopher P. Cranch, William Wetmore Story, and Thomas Hicks.
1849	Traveled through northern Italy and France to England, then returned to the United States.
1850	Gave art lessons. One of his pupils was David Johnson.
1851	Was elected an academician by the National Academy of Design.
1852–1855	Made sketching trips to the White Mountains, Niagara Falls, Canada, and Michigan. Painted literary and allegorical subjects.
1856	Sailed for England. Established himself in a studio at 2 Kensington Gate, Hyde Park South. Among his friends were John Ruskin, Sir Charles Eastlake, and Daniel Huntington.
1862	Was appointed to the American Commission of the London Exposition and received a medal from Queen Victoria for his services.
1863	Returned to New York. Visited Gettysburg to witness the aftermath of the Civil War. Resumed architectural practice.
1867	Was one of the founders of the American Water Color Society.
1869	Completed construction of his home and studio, called Aladdin, near Warwick, N.Y. Began spending summers there and winters in New York.

1878	Designed passenger stations for the Gilbert Elevated Railway in New York.
1879	Designed the decorations for the drill room of the Seventh Regiment Armory in New York.
1885	Was forced to sell Aladdin. Bought home in Hastings-on-Hudson, N.Y., and added studio; called it Ever Rest.
1885–1900	Painted mainly Hudson River scenes and worked increasingly in watercolor. Continued to exhibit at the National Academy of Design and the American Water Color Society.
1900	Died on June 22nd at Ever Rest.

Select Bibliography

BOOKS

Hartmann, Sadakichi. *A History of American Art*. 2 vols. Boston: L. C. Page & Company, 1902.

The Home Book of the Picturesque: American Scenery, Art and Literature. New York: George P. Putnam, 1852.

James, Henry. *William Wetmore Story and His Friends*. 2 vols. Boston: Houghton Mifflin & Company, 1903.

Novak, Barbara. *American Painting of the Nineteenth Century: Realism, Idealism, and the American Experience*. New York: Praeger Publishers, 1969.

———. *Nature and Culture: American Landscape and Painting, 1825–1875*. New York: Oxford University Press, 1980.

Reeves, William F. *The First Elevated Railroads in Manhattan and the Bronx of the City of New York: The Story of Their Development and Progress*. New York: The New-York Historical Society, 1936.

Talbot, William S., *Jasper F. Cropsey, 1823–1900*, Ph.D. diss., Institute of Fine Arts, New York University, 1972; published New York: Garland Publishing, 1977.

Tuckerman, Henry T. *Book of the Artists*. New York: G. P. Putnam & Sons, 1867.

CATALOGS

Adamson, Jeremy E. *Niagara: Two Centuries of Changing Attitudes, 1697–1901*. Exhibition catalog. Washington: Corcoran Gallery of Art, 1985.

Bermingham, Peter. *Jasper F. Cropsey, 1823–1900: A Retrospective View of America's Painter of Autumn*. Exhibition catalog. College Park: University of Maryland Art Gallery, 1968.

Driscoll, John P., and John K. Howat. *John Frederick Kensett: An American Master*. Exhibition catalog. Worcester: Worcester Art Museum in association with W. W. Norton & Company, New York, 1985.

M. & M. Karolik Collection of American Watercolors and Drawings. Collection catalog. Boston: Museum of Fine Arts, 1962.

Keyes, Donald D. *The White Mountains: Place and Perceptions*. Exhibition catalog. Durham: University Art Galleries, University of New Hampshire in association with the University Press of New England, Hanover, N.H., 1980.

Maddox, Kenneth W. *An Unprejudiced Eye: The Drawings of Jasper F. Cropsey*. Exhibition catalog. Yonkers: Hudson River Museum, 1979.

Novak, Barbara. *The Thyssen-Bornemisza Collection. Nineteenth-Century American Painting*. Collection catalog. New York: Vendome Press, 1986.

Rebora, Carrie. *Jasper Cropsey Watercolors*. Exhibition catalog. New York: National Academy of Design, 1985.

Talbot, William S. *Jasper F. Cropsey, 1823–1900*. Exhibition catalog. Washington: National Collection of Fine Arts, Smithsonian Institution, 1970.

PERIODICALS

Banks, William N. "Ever Rest, Jasper Francis Cropsey's House in Hastings-on-Hudson, New York." *Antiques* 130 (Nov. 1986), pp. 994–1009.

Cowdrey, Bartlett. "Jasper F. Cropsey, 1823–1900, The Colorist of the Hudson River School." *Panorama* 1 (May 1946), pp. 87–94.

Cropsey, Jasper Francis. "Up among the Clouds." *Crayon* 2 (August 8, 1855), pp. 79–80.

Forman, William H. "Jasper Francis Cropsey, N.A." *Manhattan Magazine* 3 (April 1884), pp. 372–82.

Shepherd, Barnett. "Jasper Cropsey's Staten Island Paintings, Drawings, and Architecture." *Staten Island Historian* 1, n.s., (Summer 1983), pp. 1–9.

Talbot, William S. "American Visions of Wilderness." *Cleveland Museum Bulletin* 56 (April 1969), pp. 156–59.

——— . "Jasper F. Cropsey, Child of the Hudson River School." *Antiques* 92 (Nov. 1967), pp. 713–17.

——— . "Indian Summer by Jasper F. Cropsey." *Bulletin of the Detroit Institute of Arts* 58 (1980), pp. 150–61.

UNPUBLISHED MATERIALS

Cropsey, Jasper Francis. "Reminiscences of My Own Time." Written in 1846 for C . E. Lester's *Artists of America*, 1846, but never used. Typescripts in Print Room, Museum of Fine Arts, Boston, and Newington-Cropsey Foundation coll.

——— . "Some Reflections on Natural Art: An Address for the New York Art Re-Union," Gaylords Bridge, Conn., 1845. Manuscript in Brown Reinhardt coll., Newark, Del. Typescripts in Print Room, Museum of Fine Arts, Boston, and Newington-Cropsey Foundation coll.

——— . "A Visit from Jenny Lind." Manuscript in Brown Reinhardt coll. Typescripts in Print Room, Museum of Fine Arts, Boston, and Newington-Cropsey Foundation coll.

Finney, Barbara. "Jasper F. Cropsey's Commission for the Sixth Avenue Elevated Passenger Stations (1878)." Master's thesis, George Washington University, 1983.

Miscellaneous Letters, Diaries, Sketches, and Memorandums of Jasper Francis Cropsey. Manuscripts in Newington-Cropsey Foundation coll. Microfilm in Archives of American Art, Smithsonian Institution, Washington, D.C., rolls 336–37.

Reinhardt Letters. Manuscripts in Brown Reinhardt coll. Typescripts in Newington-Cropsey Foundation coll.